SANDRA DAY
O'CONNOR

AMERICAN WOMEN of ACHIEVEMENT

SANDRA DAY O'CONNOR

PETER HUBER

CHELSEA HOUSE PUBLISHERS

NEW YORK · PHILADELPHIA

Chelsea House Publishers
EDITOR-IN-CHIEF Nancy Toff
EXECUTIVE EDITOR Remmel T. Nunn
MANAGING EDITOR Karyn Gullen Browne
COPY CHIEF Juliann Barbato
PICTURE EDITOR Adrian G. Allen
ART DIRECTOR Maria Epes
MANUFACTURING MANAGER Gerald Levine

American Women of Achievement
SENIOR EDITOR Richard Rennert

Staff for SANDRA DAY O'CONNOR
TEXT EDITOR Marian W. Taylor
COPY EDITOR Philip Koslow
DEPUTY COPY CHIEF Mark Rifkin
EDITORIAL ASSISTANT Nicole Claro
PICTURE RESEARCHER Sandy Jones
ASSISTANT ART DIRECTOR Loraine Machlin
DESIGN ASSISTANT Debora Smith
LAYOUT Ghila Krajzman
PRODUCTION MANAGER Joseph Romano
PRODUCTION COORDINATOR Marie Claire Cebrián
COVER ILLUSTRATOR Vilma Ortiz

First Printing

1 3 5 7 9 8 6 4 2

Library of Congress Cataloging-in-Publication Data

Huber, Peter W. (Peter William)
    Sandra Day O'Connor / by Peter Huber.
        p.   cm.—(American women of achievement)
    Includes bibliographical references
    Summary: Examines the life of the first woman Supreme
Court justice, including her childhood, early career, and work
as a judge.
    ISBN 1-55546-672-9
        0-7910-0448-1 (pbk.)
    1. O'Connor, Sandra Day, 1930–   —Juvenile
literature.   2. Judges—United States—Biography—Juvenile
literature.   3. United States. Supreme Court—
Biography—Juvenile litarature. [1. O'Connor, Sandra Day,
1930–   . 2. Judges.   3. United States. Supreme Court—
Biography.] I. Title.   II. Series.
KF8745.025H8   1990
347.73'2634—dc20
[B]
[347.3073534]   89-13902
[B]   CIP
[92]   AC

CONTENTS

"Remember the Ladies"—Matina S. Horner   7

1. The Right Woman   13

2. "She Held Her Own"   21

3. Wife, Mother, and Senate Majority Leader   35

4. A Formidable Judge   45

5. "Abigail Adams Would Be Pleased"   55

6. "She's Just What She Is"   69

7. "The Justice Holds the Key"   79

8. "Women Should Involve Themselves"   97

Further Reading   106

Chronology   107

Index   108

AMERICAN WOMEN OF ACHIEVEMENT

Abigail Adams
women's rights advocate

Jane Addams
social worker

Louisa May Alcott
author

Marian Anderson
singer

Susan B. Anthony
woman suffragist

Ethel Barrymore
actress

Clara Barton
founder of the American Red Cross

Elizabeth Blackwell
physician

Nellie Bly
journalist

Margaret Bourke-White
photographer

Pearl Buck
author

Rachel Carson
biologist and author

Mary Cassatt
artist

Agnes de Mille
choreographer

Emily Dickinson
poet

Isadora Duncan
dancer

Amelia Earhart
aviator

Mary Baker Eddy
founder of the Christian Science church

Betty Friedan
feminist

Althea Gibson
tennis champion

Emma Goldman
political activist

Helen Hayes
actress

Lillian Hellman
playwright

Katharine Hepburn
actress

Karen Horney
psychoanalyst

Anne Hutchinson
religious leader

Mahalia Jackson
gospel singer

Helen Keller
humanitarian

Jeane Kirkpatrick
diplomat

Emma Lazarus
poet

Clare Boothe Luce
author and diplomat

Barbara McClintock
biologist

Margaret Mead
anthropologist

Edna St. Vincent Millay
poet

Julia Morgan
architect

Grandma Moses
painter

Louise Nevelson
sculptor

Sandra Day O'Connor
Supreme Court justice

Georgia O'Keeffe
painter

Eleanor Roosevelt
diplomat and humanitarian

Wilma Rudolph
champion athlete

Florence Sabin
medical researcher

Beverly Sills
opera singer

Gertrude Stein
author

Gloria Steinem
feminist

Harriet Beecher Stowe
author and abolitionist

Mae West
entertainer

Edith Wharton
author

Phillis Wheatley
poet

Babe Didrikson Zaharias
champion athlete

CHELSEA HOUSE PUBLISHERS

"REMEMBER THE LADIES"

MATINA S. HORNER

Remember the Ladies." That is what Abigail Adams wrote to her husband, John, then a delegate to the Continental Congress, as the Founding Fathers met in Philadelphia to form a new nation in March of 1776. "Be more generous and favorable to them than your ancestors. Do not put such unlimited power in the hands of the Husbands. If particular care and attention is not paid to the Ladies," Abigail Adams warned, "we are determined to foment a Rebellion, and will not hold ourselves bound by any Laws in which we have no voice, or Representation."

The words of Abigail Adams, one of the earliest American advocates of women's rights, were prophetic. Because when we have not "remembered the ladies," they have, by their words and deeds, reminded us so forcefully of the omission that we cannot fail to remember them. For the history of American women is as interesting and varied as the history of our nation as a whole. American women have played an integral part in founding, settling, and building our country. Some we remember as remarkable women who—against great odds—achieved distinction in the public arena: Anne Hutchinson, who in the 17th century became a charismatic religious leader; Phillis Wheatley, an 18th-century black slave who became a poet; Susan B. Anthony, whose name is synonymous with the 19th-century women's rights movement and who led the struggle to enfranchise women; and, in our own century, Amelia Earhart, the first woman to cross the Atlantic Ocean by air.

7

These extraordinary women certainly merit our admiration, but other women, "common women," many of them all but forgotten, should also be recognized for their contributions to American thought and culture. Women have been community builders; they have founded schools and formed voluntary associations to help those in need; they have assumed the major responsibility for rearing children, passing on from one generation to the next the values that keep a culture alive. These and innumerable other contributions, once ignored, are now being recognized by scholars, students, and the public. It is exciting and gratifying to realize that a part of our history that was hardly acknowledged a few generations ago is now being studied and brought to light.

In recent decades, the field of women's history has grown from obscurity to a politically controversial splinter movement to academic respectability, in many cases mainstreamed into such traditional disciplines as history, economics, and psychology. Scholars of women, both female and male, have organized research centers at such prestigious institutions as Wellesley College, Stanford University, and the University of California. Other notable centers for women's studies are the Center for the American Woman and Politics at the Eagleton Institute of Politics at Rutgers University; the Henry A. Murray Research Center for the Study of Lives, at Radcliffe College; and the Women's Research and Education Institute, the research arm of the Congressional Caucus on Women's Issues. Other scholars and public figures have established archives and libraries, such as the Schlesinger Library on the History of Women in America, at Radcliffe College, and the Sophia Smith Collection, at Smith College, to collect and preserve the written and tangible legacies of women.

From the initial donation of the Women's Rights Collection in 1943, the Schlesinger Library grew to encompass vast collections documenting the manifold accomplishments of American women. Simultaneously, the women's movement in general and the academic discipline of women's studies in particular also began with a narrow definition and gradually expanded their mandate. Early causes such as woman suffrage and social reform, abolition and organized labor were joined by newer concerns such as the history of women in business and the professions and in politics and government; the study of the family; and social issues such as health policy and education.

Women, as historian Arthur M. Schlesinger, jr., once pointed out, "have constituted the most spectacular casualty of traditional history.

They have made up at least half the human race, but you could never tell that by looking at the books historians write." The new breed of historians is remedying that omission. They have written books about immigrant women and about working-class women who struggled for survival in cities and about black women who met the challenges of life in rural areas. They are telling the stories of women who, despite the barriers of tradition and economics, became lawyers and doctors and public figures.

The women's studies movement has also led scholars to question traditional interpretations of their respective disciplines. For example, the study of war has traditionally been an exercise in military and political analysis, an examination of strategies planned and executed by men. But scholars of women's history have pointed out that wars have also been periods of tremendous change and even opportunity for women, because the very absence of men on the home front enabled them to expand their educational, economic, and professional activities and to assume leadership in their homes.

The early scholars of women's history showed a unique brand of courage in choosing to investigate new subjects and take new approaches to old ones. Often, like their subjects, they endured criticism and even ostracism by their academic colleagues. But their efforts have unquestionably been worthwhile, because with the publication of each new study and book another piece of the historical patchwork is sewn into place, revealing an increasingly comprehensive picture of the role of women in our rich and varied history.

Such books on groups of women are essential, but books that focus on the lives of individuals are equally indispensable. Biographies can be inspirational, offering their readers the example of people with vision who have looked outside themselves for their goals and have often struggled against great obstacles to achieve them. Marian Anderson, for instance, had to overcome racial bigotry in order to perfect her art and perform as a concert singer. Isadora Duncan defied the rules of classical dance to find true artistic freedom. Jane Addams had to break down society's notions of the proper role for women in order to create new social institutions, notably the settlement house. All of these women had to come to terms both with themselves and with the world in which they lived. Only then could they move ahead as pioneers in their chosen callings.

Biography can inspire not only by adulation but also by realism. It helps us to see not only the qualities in others that we hope to emulate but also, perhaps, the weaknesses that made them "human." By helping us identify with the subject on a more personal level they help us to feel that we, too, can achieve such goals. We read about Eleanor Roosevelt, for example, who occupied a unique and seemingly enviable position as the wife of the president. Yet we can sympathize with her inner dilemma: an inherently shy woman who had to force herself to live a most public life in order to use her position to benefit others. We may not be able to imagine ourselves having the immense poetic talent of Emily Dickinson, but from her story we can understand the challenges faced by a creative woman who was expected to fulfill many family responsibilities. And though few of us will ever reach the level of athletic accomplishment displayed by Wilma Rudolph or Babe Zaharias, we can still appreciate their spirit, their overwhelming will to excel.

A biography is a multifaceted lens. It is first of all a magnification, the intimate examination of one particular life. But at the same time, it is a wide-angle lens, informing us about the world in which the subject lived. We come away from reading about one life knowing more about the social, political, and economic fabric of the time. It is for this reason, perhaps, that the great New England essayist Ralph Waldo Emerson wrote, in 1841, "There is properly no history: only biography." And it is also why biography, and particularly women's biography, will continue to fascinate writers and readers alike.

SANDRA DAY
O'CONNOR

Arizona Court of Appeals judge Sandra Day O'Connor gives an interview on July 8, 1981, one day after her historic nomination to the U.S. Supreme Court.

ONE

The Right Woman

On June 17, 1981, Sandra Day O'Connor glanced at the front page of her local newspaper, then read it with increasing interest. According to the *Arizona Republic*, Supreme Court justice Potter Stewart had just announced his retirement. Arizona senator Dennis DeConcini, said the *Republic*, had suggested that President Ronald Reagan replace Justice Stewart with a 51-year-old judge on the Arizona Court of Appeals. Her name: Sandra Day O'Connor.

O'Connor knew that senators often proposed people from their own states to fill court vacancies. She also knew that presidents rarely heeded such advice, particularly when it concerned a rare and all-important appointment to the United States Supreme Court. During his 1980 campaign for the presidency, Reagan had promised to appoint a woman to the Court, a move that would shatter an almost 200-year-old tradition. Still, O'Connor later recalled, she regarded De Concini's suggestion as no more than a friendly gesture from a fellow Arizonan. Eight days later, she would find she had been mistaken.

In April, when he learned of Stewart's plan to retire, the president had asked aides to compile a list of the nation's most prominent female lawyers and judges. Topping the completed list was the name of Sandra Day O'Connor. Reagan then ordered the Justice Department to begin a secret investigation of the Arizona judge's past and present activities. Receiving a positive report, he told Attorney General William French Smith to call O'Connor. Smith telephoned her on June 25 and, two days later, sent his top deputies to interview her in Phoenix.

O'Connor held several lengthy conversations with Smith's chief counselor and his staff. They returned with glowing accounts. "She really made it easy," said one official later. "She was the right age, had the right philosophy, the right combination of experience, the right political affiliation, the right backing." On July 1, O'Connor quietly met with Reagan in the Oval Office of the White House. After a 45-minute talk with her, Reagan reportedly told aides he would interview no further candidates for the Supreme Court vacancy: O'Connor, he said, was the right woman for the job.

Getting wind of her possible nomination, reporters besieged O'Connor with calls, but the judge remained politely silent. Both O'Connor and the now real possibility of a historic break with tradition were suddenly hot topics among the nation's columnists, television commentators, government officials, and private citizens. Reagan ended days of public speculation with a televised press conference on July 7.

"Without doubt," said the president, "the most awesome appointment a

Gathered at the Arizona Court of Appeals for a 1981 family portrait are O'Connor; her husband, John; and her sons (left to right) Jay, Brian, and Scott.

Senator Dennis DeConcini (left) defends O'Connor's Supreme Court nomination during a televised debate with National Right to Life Committee president J. C. Wilkie in July 1981.

president can make is to the United States Supreme Court." Recalling his campaign promise to appoint a woman, he added, "That is not to say I would appoint a woman merely to do so. That would not be fair to women, nor to future generations of all Americans whose lives are so deeply affected by decisions of the Court. Rather, I pledged to appoint a woman who meets the very high standards I demand of all court appointees."

Reagan then introduced O'Connor, whom he described as "truly a 'person

for all seasons,' possessing those unique qualities of temperament, fairness, intellectual capacity and devotion to the public good which have characterized the 101 'brethren' who have preceded her." (The term *brethren*, or "brothers," had been traditionally applied to the Court's exclusively male justices.)

The official nomination sparked a noisy public debate. Most of Reagan's deeply conservative supporters opposed O'Connor; her record, said right-wing Republicans, showed an alarmingly lib-

15

eral tinge. And because she had taken a moderate view of abortion when she served as an Arizona state legislator, antiabortion activists vowed to fight her confirmation. "We feel we've been betrayed," asserted a spokesman for the Life Amendment Political Action Committee. The Reverend Jerry Falwell, leader of the fundamentalist Moral Majority, said all "good Christians" should think twice about Sandra Day O'Connor.

Most of the nation's prominent women's groups, however, approved of the Arizona judge. Eleanor Smeal of the National Organization for Women called the nomination "a major victory for women's rights." And Massachusetts's liberal Democratic senator, Edward Kennedy, expressed admiration for the Republican nominee: "Every American," said Kennedy, "can take pride in the president's commitment to select such a woman for this critical office." Both sides—pro- and anti-O'Connor—staged Washington demonstrations, and both appeared at her confirmation hearings before the Senate Judiciary Committee.

Although the Constitution empowers the president to nominate federal judges, candidates must be approved by the Senate before taking office. O'Connor's three-day confirmation hearings attracted a record number of journalists, witnesses, and spectators. All listened attentively as she read her opening statement. "As the first woman to be nominated as a Supreme Court justice, I am particularly honored," she said, "but I happily share the honor with millions of American women of yesterday and today whose abilities and conduct have given me this opportunity for service." Expressing her lifelong "reverence and respect" for the Court, O'Connor said, "It is to the United States Supreme Court that we all turn when we seek that which we want most from our government: equal justice under law."

Sessions with the Senate Judiciary Committee can be harrowing. Faced with blunt, sometimes hostile questions, federal nominees have been known to lose their temper, to contradict themselves, or to misstate their own positions. O'Connor did none of these things. She calmly discussed her beliefs about the law, stating that, in her opinion, "judges should avoid substituting their own views . . . for those of the legislature." Elected legislators, she maintained, are more "attuned to the public will" and more "politically accountable" than appointed judges. She also discussed her own experiences and recounted some of the prejudices she had encountered as a newly graduated female lawyer in the 1950s.

But O'Connor steadfastly refused to predict how she would vote as a Supreme Court justice, particularly on the politically sensitive issue of abortion. Despite her firm stand, and despite the vehement protests of the political Right, O'Connor won the approval of 17 of the committee's 18 members. A few days later, the full Senate confirmed her as an associate justice of the Supreme Court. The vote was 99–0.

After discussing her upcoming confirmation hearings, O'Connor leaves the Justice Department in Washington, D.C., with Attorney General William French Smith.

On the afternoon of September 25, 1981, every spectator's seat in the United States Supreme Court was filled. At 2:04, the doors at either side of the chamber swung open, sending an expectant murmur through the crowd. The president of the United States emerged from one door. From the other strode Sandra Day O'Connor, ready to take her oath as the 102nd member of the Supreme Court—and the first woman in its 191-year history.

After Reagan and O'Connor had taken their place, the Court clerk issued his traditional order: "All rise!" Everyone in the courtroom, including O'Connor and Reagan, stood as the Court's eight black-robed justices approached their imposing mahogany bench. Seated at its center, Chief Justice Warren E. Burger accepted the presidential document that commissioned Sandra Day O'Connor an associate justice of the Supreme Court.

Ready to face the Senate Judiciary Committee, Sandra Day O'Connor exchanges a good-luck kiss with her husband, John Jay O'Connor III.

The Supreme Court meets in this massive white marble building in Washington, D.C. Carved above the entrance is the Court's great motto: Equal Justice Under Law.

O'Connor placed her hand on a Bible and repeated the time-honored words of fidelity to country and Court: "I, Sandra Day O'Connor, do solemnly swear that I will support and defend the Constitution of the United States against all enemies, foreign and domestic; that I will bear true faith and allegiance to the same; that I take this obligation freely, without any mental reservation or purpose of evasion; and that I will well and faithfully discharge the duties of the office on which I am about to enter. So help me God."

Completing the oath, O'Connor donned a black robe. Then, as her family, friends, and hundreds of Washington officials watched, she walked to the far-right side of the bench—the position traditionally reserved for the Court's newest justice—and joined the highest court in the land.

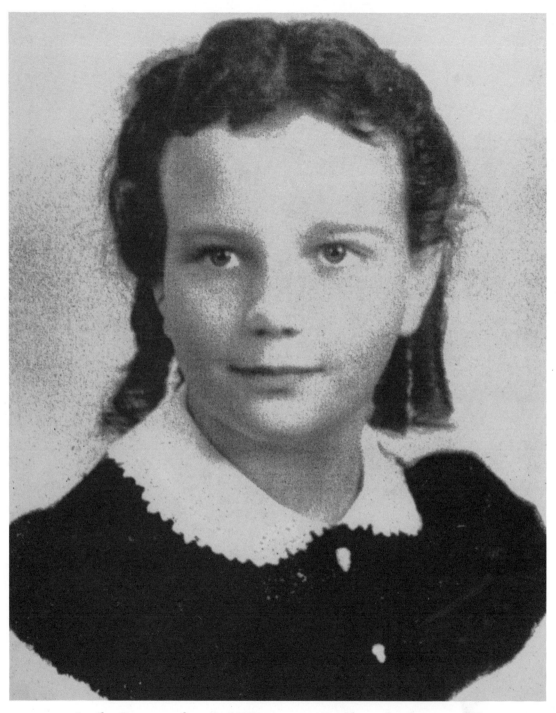

Sandra Day, seen here in 1938, spent most of her school years in El Paso, Texas. She later confessed that when she was away from the Lazy B ranch, she was "always homesick."

TWO

"She Held Her Own"

Sandra Day, the first child of Ada Mae and Harry Day, was born in El Paso, Texas, on March 26, 1930. She spent her early years at the Lazy B, the family cattle ranch on the Arizona–New Mexico border. Sandra's paternal grandparents, Alice and Henry Clay ("H. C.") Day, had founded the ranch in 1880. Leaving his native Vermont in the mid-1870s, H. C. Day had settled in Wichita, Kansas, where he met and married Alice Edith Hilton. After establishing a successful lumber business, Day and his wife moved farther west, to Pasadena, California.

In the post–Civil War years, an enterprising settler could buy public lands at very low cost; for a small investment, H. C. Day acquired a 300-square-mile tract of harsh desert land in Arizona Territory. For $50,000, he imported 5,000 head of cattle from Mexico. The animals, already branded with a sideways, or "lazy" letter *B*, gave the ranch its name.

Day had originally planned to remain in California, leaving the ranch in the hands of a foreman. He soon learned, however, that the man he had hired was stealing from him, putting his own brand on cattle that belonged to the Lazy B. The Days then moved in to manage the ranch themselves. H. C. Day built a small house, planted orchards, and constructed a schoolhouse for his children. The cowboys who worked for him built a four-room adobe (sun-dried clay) house. Like other homes of the time and place, this one had no running water, indoor plumbing, or electricity.

In the 1880s, life in the Southwest presented many challenges: dusty, dry land, unpredictable weather, no neighbors within miles. Adding to the settlers' hardships were the Apache

H. C. Day, Sandra's grandfather, sits for a portrait with two friends in the 1880s. A native of Vermont, Day had headed west in the mid-1870s.

Geronimo and his followers. But despite the hazards of their frontier existence, the Days loved their huge, remote spread. As one of their descendants put it many years later, "This dried-up old piece of land is what we are."

In 1899, the Days' fifth and last child, Harry, was born. H. C. Day knew that the ranch's one-room schoolhouse could offer only a makeshift education, so when Harry was ready for grade school, his father returned with his family to Pasadena, once more leaving the ranch under the management of a foreman. After high school, Harry planned to attend Stanford University, near San Francisco, but his hopes were cut short when his father died suddenly. Learning that the ranch was in serious financial trouble, the young man abandoned the thought of college and returned to the Lazy B. He spent the next 10 years settling the claims of creditors and putting the ranch back on its feet.

Eager to increase his herd, Harry Day arranged to buy some stock from Willis Wilkey, a cattle dealer in El Paso, Texas. There, he met Wilkey's daughter, Ada Mae. A 1925 graduate of the University of Arizona, Ada Mae Wilkey was a sophisticated young woman with a keen eye for fashion, a deep interest in literature, and a solid reputation as a vocalist and pianist. Harry Day "liked to say he met my mother when he went to buy some bulls from her father and she was part of the deal," joked Sandra Day O'Connor years later. "This," she added quickly, "is not true, of course."

Indians. Resentful about being driven from their ancestral lands, the Apaches, led by their legendary chief, Geronimo, staged frequent raids on the area's ranches in 1885 and 1886. Although no one at the Lazy B was harmed, Alice and H. C. Day lost several horses to

What is true is that Harry Day and Ada Mae Wilkey fell in love. Letters soon began to fly between the Lazy B and El Paso, and Harry Day made the 200-mile trip to the Texas city whenever he could manage a free weekend. In 1927, after several months of long-distance courtship, the young couple eloped to Las Cruces, New Mexico, then settled down in the little adobe house at the Lazy B. The city-raised bride learned that ranch life meant hard work, but she adjusted quickly. Ada Mae Day cooked, cleaned, and carried water, not only for herself and her husband but also for the four cowhands who shared their small house.

Both Days were innovative: Harry built some of the nation's first solar heaters, and Ada Mae kept up with the world by subscribing to the *Los Angeles Times*, *Vogue*, and the *New Yorker*. Three years after their marriage, Ada Mae Day gave birth to her first child, Sandra.

Growing up on the isolated ranch, Sandra had no friends her own age. She spent her early years trotting along behind her father and learning the rancher's trade. By the time she was eight years old, she could brand cattle, ride a horse, drive a tractor, and fire a rifle with accuracy. Harry Day, a family friend later recalled, "expected everybody to keep the critter population down by shooting jack rabbits, prairie dogs, coyotes, rattlesnakes, Gila monsters—anything that ate his pasture grass or went after his cattle."

Sandra was the youngest "cowboy" at the Lazy B. She was also the youngest

Ada Mae Day and her husband, Harry, take their one-year-old daughter for a stroll around the ranch. Sandra was an only child until she was eight.

reader: Tutored by her mother, she had learned to read at four. In the evenings, Ada Mae Day read to her daughter, using the *Book of Knowledge* encyclopedia, the *Saturday Evening Post*, and *National Geographic* magazine as storybooks.

23

Sandra rides her favorite horse, Chico, at the Lazy B. By the age of 10, the young "cowboy" was an expert at riding, shooting, branding cattle, and driving a tractor.

But Ada Mae Day realized she could not satisfy her daughter's irrepressible curiosity indefinitely. The child needed formal education, and the area offered no adequate schools. Thus, when Sandra reached the age of six, her parents sent her to live with her maternal grandparents in El Paso, where first-rate schooling was available. "We missed her terribly, and she missed us," said Ada Mae Day later, "but there was no other way for her to get a good education."

Sandra's grandfather, Willis Wilkey, was in poor health, but Grandmother Mamie Scott Wilkey had no trouble managing her household. With her husband, she had come out West in a covered wagon and built a new life from scratch. A strong-willed, self-sufficient woman, Mamie Scott Wilkey had already sent her daughter to college, and she expected the best from her granddaughter as well.

At the Lazy B, ranch business had often interrupted Sandra's lessons, but her grandmother's careful supervision brought structure and discipline to her education. As an adult, Sandra Day recalled Mamie Scott Wilkey as the woman who most influenced her life. "She was a wonderful person—very supportive of me," said her granddaughter. "She would always tell me that I could do anything I wanted to do. She was convinced of that, and it was very encouraging."

Mamie Wilkey sent Sandra to the Radford School for Girls, an exclusive private institution in El Paso. Also enrolled at Radford was Sandra's cousin

24

Sandra Day (left) and her cousin Flournoy Davis model matching dresses in about 1940. The daughter of Ada Mae Day's sister, Flournoy became Sandra's best friend.

Flournoy Davis, who soon became her best friend. When Sandra returned to the Lazy B during summer vacations, Flournoy often went with her. The girls spent their holidays swimming, riding, and helping the cowboys with ranch chores. "We played with dolls," Flournoy Davis Manzo told a reporter in 1981, "but we knew what to do with screwdrivers and nails too. Living on a ranch made us very self-sufficient." Recalling young Sandra many years later, one of the Lazy B hands said, "She wasn't the rough and rugged type, but she worked well with us in the canyons—she held her own."

Sandra and Flournoy hated to go back to school in the fall and dreaded the grueling trip to El Paso. When vacation ended, the two often hid. "One time," recalled Harry Day later, "[they] were swimming in the water tank and refused to come out. I got a lariat and roped them both out of the water. 'Back to school with you girls,' I said."

When Sandra was in third grade, her grandfather died, but she continued to live with her grandmother during the school year. After her husband's death, Mamie Wilkey spent summers with the Days at the Lazy B. Sandra was an only child until 1938, when her sister, Ann, was born. A brother, Alan, arrived in 1939. Now she desperately wanted to stay with her family all year, and her parents finally agreed. She enrolled in eighth grade at a school in the town of Lordsburg, some 22 miles from the ranch. But the hours she spent on the road each day proved exhausting, and after a year, Sandra returned to her old

Observed by her parents and a visiting friend, Sandra pats a bull at the Lazy B. Sandra was not "the rugged type," a ranch hand later recalled, "but she held her own."

routine: She spent the school months at the Radford School in El Paso and the summers back at the ranch. "I was always homesick when I wasn't there," she admitted later.

With the arrival of Ann and Alan, Sandra looked forward to summers more than ever. Her siblings have described her as a gentle but firm big sister. "When she said something," Alan Day once recalled, "we did it."

On one occasion, Sandra caught her little brother smoking in a haystack; it turned out to be his first and last experiment with tobacco. But despite Sandra's occasional big-sister bossiness, the three Day children got along well. They particularly enjoyed their summer travels together.

Eager for their youngsters to see the world outside the Lazy B, Ada Mae and Harry Day planned annual family expe-

*Ada Mae Day joins her children for a portrait on Easter Day, 1940.
Sandra cuddles her two-year-old sister, Ann; their mother holds Alan,
aged one.*

ditions that took them as far afield as
Alaska, Cuba, Honduras, and Mexico.
"One day when Sandra was 14," her
brother later recalled, "[our parents]
packed us into the car and we drove to
every state capital west of the Mississippi. We climbed to the dome of every
capitol building until finally we had to
come home."

When Sandra returned to Radford after her year's absence, the Radford staff
decided she was ready for high school.
Skipping a grade, she graduated from
Radford at the age of 12, then enrolled
in El Paso's Austin High School. "Sandra always knew how to handle herself," one of her high school friends,
Hondey Hill McAlmon, recalled later.
"She was in honors classes and was
terrific at impromptu [unrehearsed]
speaking, but she also did all the nor-
mal things teenagers did—had crushes

27

and talked about boys. She was just never loud or awkward. I was never jealous of her, but I do remember feeling a little inferior. She really could do everything well." Sandra Day did everything so well, in fact, that she graduated from Austin High at 16.

Intending to continue her education, Day applied to Stanford University, the college her father had dreamed of attending three decades earlier. In 1946, however, the nation's schools were flooded with applications from newly returned World War II veterans. Gaining admittance to any university was difficult for a woman; getting accepted by Stanford, where men outnumbered women by five to two, was even harder.

Day was younger than most college applicants and had no family connections with Stanford. Her chances of attending the prestigious university, said advisers, seemed slight. But nothing discouraged the energetic young woman from the Lazy B. "I only applied to Stanford and no place else," she recalled later. To the happy surprise of family and friends, her confidence proved justified. The Stanford University admissions committee accepted 16-year-old Sandra Day for its 1946 freshman class.

Sandra Day, recalled her college roommate, Marilyn Brown, was "very shy" but "easy to get along with." Talking to a *New York Times* reporter in 1981, Brown said, "Even though she was younger than us, she always seemed to handle it. She never got upset. She never went into a panic about anything. And she was fun." San-

Day, pictured here in the Stanford University yearbook, had already entered law school when she received her undergraduate degree in 1950.

dra Day was also intense, ambitious, and hardworking.

In the 1940s, an era when many American college women shied away from "men's subjects," most female students majored in English or education. Sandra Day picked economics. She worked hard and earned excellent grades, both in economics and in business law, one of the subjects included in her major. Intrigued by the concept of legal reasoning, Day decided to pursue the study of law. Stanford offered a "three-three" program, which enabled a student to earn both a bachelor's degree and a law degree in six years instead of the customary seven. In 1950, when Day graduated magna cum laude (with high honor) from Stanford University, she had already finished her first year at Stanford Law School.

Like most American law schools, Stanford used the *Socratic method*, a system of study and instruction that teaches students to think quickly under pressure. Rather than relying only on lectures and textbooks, the Socratic method requires students to study actual cases and the opinions of the judges who presided over them. Then, in class, the students are subjected to surprise cross-examinations by their professor, much as a lawyer is questioned by a Supreme Court justice.

Law students might, for example, examine the 19th-century case of a young Illinois woman named Myra Bradwell. Determined to become the first female attorney in the state, Bradwell studied law, then applied for a state license. (Like a doctor, a lawyer must acquire an official state license before he or she may practice in any given state.) Although Bradwell presented the Illinois licensing board—made up of two justices from the state supreme court—with all the proper papers, she was refused a license. Illinois had no law prohibiting women from entering the legal profession; the justices simply believed that women should not practice law.

Bradwell then filed a suit with the Illinois Supreme Court itself. No surprise here; the court rejected Bradwell's plea. "God designed the sexes to occupy different spheres of action," wrote the Illinois chief justice, who held that only men were fit to "make, apply, and execute" the law. Bradwell next brought her plea to the United States Supreme Court. Through her lawyer, she argued that the Constitution's Fourteenth Amendment, which calls for equal protection of all citizens under the law, prohibited discrimination against women in this way.

In 1872, the Court ruled, 8–1, against Bradwell. "Man is, or should be, women's protector and defender," wrote Justice Joseph P. Bradley. "The natural and proper timidity and delicacy which belongs to the fair sex evidently unfits it for many of the occupations of civil life." The practice of law, continued the justice, required "the decision and firmness which are presumed to predominate in the sterner sex."

Teaching by the Socratic method, a law school professor might assign the Bradwell case, then call randomly on a student during class. "Miss Day," the instructor might ask, "what provision of the Constitution was involved in the Bradwell case? The Fourteenth Amendment, you say? Which clause of that amendment? Can *Bradwell* be distinguished from a case involving discrimination by race? If women can be kept out of the legal profession, can men be kept out of nursing? Is it legal for an insurance company to charge women drivers lower rates than men because women have safer driving records?"

The professor would ask one question after another, teasing out fine dis-

Stanford Law School's class of 1952 contains two future Supreme Court justices: Sandra Day is in the first row, second from left; William Rehnquist is at far left in the back row.

tinctions in the law. The student would need to think fast, answer the questions, explain her reasoning, argue for one rule or another. She would have read the case and thought about the issues, but she would not know what questions would be asked, or of whom, until the moment arrived. The scene would be played in front of dozens of other students, all scribbling notes and trying to think of the answers themselves.

In many ways, a law school classroom imitates a real courtroom. Indeed, arguments before the Supreme Court proceed in much the same way as law school examinations, although at the Court, nine justices fire the questions at one lonely lawyer. The secret to surviving this kind of ordeal, whether in law school or the courtroom, is to arrive very well prepared. At Stanford, Sandra Day was just that.

"I think that anything you do in life requires preparation," she told an interviewer years later. "And if you are prepared and have thought about it, then things won't be a problem. If you feel you are not prepared, that's grounds for concern." At Stanford, teachers soon recognized Day as an extraordinarily well suited candidate for the law. She was elected to the prestigious Order of the Coif, an honorary legal society, and she was named an editor of the *Stanford Law Review*.

Among law students, it is a high honor to be chosen to work on a review, a publication that discusses cases and trends in legal thinking. A law review's principal articles are written by professors and practicing lawyers, but students select, edit, and check the articles. Student editors spend countless hours in the law library, poring over footnotes and researching opinions. It is hard work, but it teaches the meticulous practice of law. And by working on such projects together, students learn from each other as well as from the authors whose articles they edit.

Her job on the *Stanford Law Review* brought Sandra Day more than legal expertise. One evening, checking material for an upcoming article, she went to the law library. There, she met another student editor, assigned to the same piece. John Jay O'Connor III, a member of the class behind Day's, asked her out for dinner, and she accepted. It was to be the first of many shared experiences. The couple dated for the next two years, during which time Day brought O'Connor home to meet her family at the Lazy B. They approved of her taste. "We liked John," Harry Day joked later, "but I've seen better cowboys."

In June 1952, Sandra Day graduated third in her law school class. Outnum-

Following tradition, Sandra Day O'Connor offers her bridegroom a slice of wedding cake. The O'Connors were married at the Lazy B in 1952.

bered by male students 30 to 1, she had scored higher than all but 2 members of her class. One of them was William H. Rehnquist, a young man who would later become chief justice of the U.S. Supreme Court.

On December 20, 1952, six months after her graduation, Sandra Day married John O'Connor. Following the wedding, which was attended by 200 guests at the Lazy B ranch, the O'Connors returned to Stanford, where John O'Connor would complete his final semester of law school. Sandra O'Connor started to look for a job at once, but despite her excellent academic credentials, she met with no success.

"I interviewed with law firms in Los Angeles and San Francisco," O'Connor recalled later, "but none had ever hired a woman before as a lawyer, and they were not prepared to do so." She finally got one job offer, from Gibson, Dunn & Crutcher in Los Angeles—to work as a legal secretary. Ironically, one of the law firm's partners was future United States attorney general William French Smith, the man who would one day advise the president of the United States to appoint Sandra Day O'Connor to the Supreme Court.

But that was far in the future. For the moment, O'Connor kept looking for work. Because the public-service area offered the best opportunities to female lawyers, she centered her search on a government job. She finally found work as a law clerk in the office of the San Mateo, California, county attorney. She loved the job and was soon promoted to deputy county attorney. "I think that in public employment one often gets more responsibility earlier than one does in the private sector," she remarked later. Her first job, she said, "influenced the balance of my life because it demonstrated how much I did enjoy public service."

Appointed to the Arizona state senate in 1969, 39-year-old Sandra O'Connor quickly earned a reputation as "a perfectionist rooted in the law."

T H R E E

Wife, Mother, and Senate Majority Leader

In June 1953, Sandra O'Connor left her San Mateo job and went to Germany with her husband. After graduating from law school, John O'Connor had been drafted into the army (the United States was still involved in the Korean War). Assigned to the Judge Advocate General's Corps (the army's legal division), O'Connor was sent to Frankfurt, West Germany. There, Sandra O'Connor found employment as a civilian lawyer for the Quartermaster Corps, which buys the army's food and equipment and sells surplus supplies. It was her job to check military contracts and to deal with any legal problems they presented.

The O'Connors spent their free time in Europe traveling and skiing. They visited 14 countries, touring the museums and cathedrals of the Continent's great capitals. For their last three months in Europe, they rented a chalet in the Austrian Alps, where they spent most of their time skiing. (The sport remains a favorite pastime of the couple, who often spend their vacations skiing near Park City, Utah.)

After John O'Connor's tour of duty ended in December 1956, he and his wife returned to the United States. They bought a plot of land and began building a new house in Phoenix, Arizona, a rapidly developing urban area where they hoped to become active in community affairs. Both passed the state bar examination and were admitted to law practice in Arizona. John O'Connor took a job with Fennemore, Craig, von Ammon, and Udall, a prosperous Phoenix law firm. Sandra O'Connor's life, however, took a differ-

The O'Connors enjoy a Colorado ski vacation with their son Scott in 1979. Always avid skiers, Sandra and John O'Connor spent months on the Alpine slopes in 1956.

ent path for the moment. On October 8, 1957, she gave birth to her first child, Scott Hampton O'Connor.

O'Connor was delighted with her new son, but she still wanted to keep one foot in the legal profession. She looked for a part-time job that would let her spend half of each day with her baby. Because this plan ruled out major law firms—few of which hired women in any case—she decided to start a private practice with another young lawyer. In 1958, she and Tom Tobin, who had passed the Arizona bar examination on the same day as the O'Connors, opened an office in the Phoenix suburb of Maryvale. She spent mornings in the office and the rest of each day with Scott.

At the new firm, O'Connor later recalled, "we did whatever business we could get to come our way. We had a diverse, small-town type of practice. We took landlord-tenant, domestic, small-business and even criminal appointments on occasion to help pay the rent." O'Connor and Tobin also represented people charged with crimes but unable to afford lawyers. As court-appointed attorneys for the poor, O'Connor and her partner were paid by the state.

When her second son, Brian, arrived in January 1960, O'Connor decided to stop practicing law for a while and concentrate on her family. In May 1962, she gave birth to a third son, Jay. It would be three years before she returned to the practice of law, but she expressed no resentment about staying home with her husband and children. "Marriage is far more than an exchange of vows," she once observed. "It is the foundation of the family, mankind's basic unit of society, the hope of the world, and the strength of our country. It is the relationship between ourselves and the generations that follow."

Nevertheless, she noted later, "There was never a doubt in my mind about wanting to have a career as well as a family. Life is just more interesting if one is engaged in intellectually stimulating work." Even when her children were very young, O'Connor maintained her contacts with the legal world through volunteer work: She organized a lawyer-referral plan for the county bar association, took assignments as trustee in bankruptcy estates, and served as a juvenile-court referee.

O'Connor also worked for a variety of local organizations, including the YMCA and the Phoenix Historical Society. "I have always wanted to be actively involved in the community in which I lived," O'Connor said later, "and to participate in making some of the decisions—political, economic, and cultural—about that community. I have wanted to be part of the process of the dynamics of my community, to help it develop and achieve its goals, to try to make it a good place to live."

Under the leadership of conservative Republican U.S. senator Barry Goldwater, the Republican party was fast gaining ground in Arizona's cities. In the early 1960s, Sandra O'Connor joined the party and plunged into local political work. At the same time, her husband became president of the Maricopa County Young Republicans Club and a member of the local zoning and planning commission and the hospital advisory board.

Despite her responsibilities at home, Sandra O'Connor pursued her political interests with enthusiasm and energy. She served as a county precinct committee member for the Republican party from 1960 to 1964, as legislative district chair from 1962 to 1965, and as vice-chair of the Maricopa County Republican Committee in 1964. She was also appointed to the Maricopa Board of Adjustments and Appeals, the Governor's Commission on Marriage and the Family, and the Arizona State Personnel Commission.

In 1965, when her youngest son turned three, O'Connor decided to re-enter the legal profession. A call to the office of the Arizona attorney general produced a part-time job as a state assistant attorney general. As her sons grew older, she gradually took on more and more responsibilities; in a few years, she found herself once again doing full-time legal work along with caring for her family. But not even two jobs seemed to be enough for Sandra O'Connor; she also remained active in Republican politics.

In 1966, after several decades of Democratic dominance, the Republicans elected a governor and won control of both houses of the Arizona state legislature. Three years later, the state senator from the O'Connors' district left the Arizona legislature for a position in President Richard Nixon's administration. The Arizona Republican party offered the vacated seat to one of its most dedicated and hardworking members: Sandra Day O'Connor. Although the post paid only $6,000 per year, John O'Connor's salary was more than enough to support the family, and Sandra O'Connor gladly accepted the offer.

It was a good time for a woman to be entering politics. As the women's movement made inroads in the nation's consciousness, women across the country were demanding equal access to the work force and equal treatment under the law. Responding to mounting pressure from women and racial minorities, Congress had passed the Equal Pay Act of 1963 and Title VII of the Civil Rights Act of 1964, which prohibited employment discrimination on the basis of race or sex.

When O'Connor took her seat in the Arizona legislature (where she was one of only two woman senators), reporters asked her to define her positions: She was, she replied, "a fiscal [financial] conservative and a moderate Republican." O'Connor soon proved the description accurate. As one Democratic state senator put it, "She's certainly a conservative in the conventional sense, but beyond that, she's extremely fair." O'Connor, added her colleague, was "a perfectionist rooted in the law." One year after her appointment to the state senate, O'Connor ran for reelection and won. Two years later, she was elected to a second full term. In that year, 1972, she also served as a state cochair of the Committee to Reelect the President, Richard Nixon.

Shortly after the 1972 campaign, Arizona Republicans gathered to select their senate majority leader. It is the leader's job to coordinate bills, line up support for party goals, organize legislative committees, and generally keep the peace among the party faithful and their often conflicting desires and priorities. As their leader the Republicans chose Sandra Day O'Connor, making her the first woman to serve as majority leader in any state senate in the nation. It was a case, said one colleague, of "talent winning out."

When she opened the 1973 legislative session, O'Connor made it clear that gender would have no bearing on her role. "I think my job as a legislative leader will be no different because I am a woman," she said, "than it would be if I were a man." In her new position, O'Connor earned good marks from her fellow legislators. "She was a super floor leader," said one colleague. "She was devoted to the law by the nature of her own professionalism and was extraordinarily thorough in drafting legislation."

Reporting on O'Connor's performance in the legislature, *Time* magazine observed that her "devotion to detail soon became legendary." The majority leader, reported the magazine, once offered an amendment to a bill to insert a single comma—a bit of punctuation that made the legislation's intent unmistakable. "As majority leader," said *Time*, "she learned to use both tact and toughness to cajole colleagues into reaching consensus on divisive issues." Said a local reporter: "With her, it was 'push or pull or get the hell out of the way.'"

In 1974, O'Connor ended the year's legislative session without quite satisfying all her colleagues. Furious be-

Heavy traffic moves through downtown Phoenix in the mid-1950s. O'Connor and her husband settled in the rapidly growing Arizona city in 1957.

Members of the National Organization for Women demonstrate for the Equal Rights Amendment (ERA) in front of the White House in 1969. O'Connor was an early ERA supporter.

cause his pet project had failed to reach the senate floor, one committee chairman approached the floor leader and growled, "If you were a man, I'd punch you in the mouth." Unflappable as always, O'Connor smiled sweetly. "If you were a man," she said, "you could."

Alfredo Gutierrez, a Democratic Arizona state senator, frequently opposed O'Connor, but he gave her full credit as a political leader. "She worked interminable hours and read everything there was," Gutierrez later told a reporter. "It was impossible to win a debate with her. We [the Democrats] would go on

40

the floor with a few facts and let rhetoric [speechmaking] do the rest. Not Sandy. She would overwhelm you with her knowledge."

O'Connor's voting record in the Arizona legislature reflected her conservative outlook, but it also showed support for a number of liberal measures. Speaking to a reporter in 1981, David Tierney, a Phoenix attorney and longtime O'Connor acquaintance, called her "a middle-roader—not an extreme rightist or an extreme leftist." In short, asserted Tierney, Sandra Day O'Connor was "her own person." On the conservative side, Senator O'Connor opposed gun control and school busing to promote integration. And she helped write the bill that reinstated the death penalty in Arizona.

On the other side of the political spectrum, O'Connor supported bilingual education in the state, whose Hispanic population had rapidly increased. She also helped pass a tough antipollution law and endorsed on-the-job accident insurance for migrant workers. She worked for laws that provided regular reviews for people involuntarily committed to mental institutions; for laws that reformed state regulations on inheritances, wills, and estates; and for modernized divorce laws. And, although her own children attended private schools, O'Connor opposed state aid to nonpublic schools.

When it came to the sensitive issue of abortion, O'Connor demonstrated her characteristic "middle-roader" attitude. She supported one bill that restricted Arizona state funds for abortions for poor women and another that gave hospital personnel the legal right to refuse to participate in abortions. In 1973, however, she took a position that angered members of the right-to-life movement. In this case, she supported a bill that would have made "all medically acceptable family-planning methods and information" available to any individual who wanted them. Responding to criticism of her position, O'Connor asserted that her "family-planning" program did not include abortion, which, she said later, she found "personally repugnant."

The Equal Rights Amendment (ERA) was another issue on which O'Connor displeased right-wing Republicans. First introduced in 1923, this proposed constitutional change states: "Equality of rights under the law shall not be denied or abridged by the United States or by any state on account of sex." Congress finally passed the ERA in 1972, but before it could become part of the Constitution, it needed ratification (approval) by three-fourths of the states.

When the ERA came before the Arizona legislature in 1972, O'Connor urged its passage. "Women," she said firmly, "have lacked a certain amount of job opportunity and have failed to receive equal pay for equal work." But despite O'Connor's support, the ERA ratification bill failed to pass. Then, in 1974, O'Connor coauthored a resolution that called for an Arizona referendum, or popular vote, on the ERA. The resolution met defeat. (The ERA campaign would also lose, at least for the moment, in June 1982. At that point, the deadline for state ratification passed with only 35 of the needed 38 states approving the proposed amendment.) After 1974, O'Connor discontinued her public support for the ERA, deciding that equality for women could be achieved through other channels.

Although she solidly supported equal job opportunities for women, O'Connor also endorsed traditional personal values. In 1970, a time when some people called marriage old-fashioned and the brassiere a symbol of female oppression, O'Connor addressed a group of Arizona high school students. "I come to you tonight," she announced, "wearing my bra and my wedding band."

Jokes about underwear and wedding rings aside, however, O'Connor be-

Celebrating the Senate's extension of the ERA ratification deadline, jubilant women gather outside the U.S. Capitol in 1978. The proposed amendment died four years later.

lieved that women were all too often held back by the law, sometimes openly, sometimes in more subtle ways. "In family law, property law, and elsewhere," she said, "women, particularly black women, [are] relegated to a position that could best be described as second class." Laws that affected women became her specific interest. One Arizona statute, for example, prohibited women from working more than eight hours per day. Supposedly enacted to protect women, the law actually discriminated against them. Sandra O'Connor realized that neither she nor millions of other ambitious American women could achieve professional success by working a mere 40-hour week. Thanks to O'Connor's efforts, the Arizona "women's-work" law was repealed.

O'Connor also worked to change the state law on community property (goods owned jointly by a wife and husband). Under Arizona law, a husband had all power to manage and control such property. O'Connor was determined to bring about a major change in this situation. "She got together a committee of legislators, lawyers, business people, and women's rights people," recalled Alice Bendheim, a Phoenix attorney who collaborated on the reform. "She made it a noncontroversial bill—a part of the marriage and divorce law—and she shepherded it through the Senate in a very shrewd way. It passed without fanfare, which is the only way it could have passed."

Sandra O'Connor's experience in the

Palm trees line the entrance to the State Capitol in Phoenix. O'Connor's years in the Arizona legislature deepened her lifelong respect for state government.

Arizona legislature gave her rich insights into the complexities of state politics. It also helped shape her philosophy about state and federal power. The "state legislatures are closest to the people and reflect their will in the most direct manner," she observed later. "The independence of the states," she added, "helps to protect one of our most cherished liberties: the right to govern ourselves."

Attorney John O'Connor joins Judge Sandra O'Connor at her Arizona Court of Appeals office. Shelves at rear hold the judge's gavel and her multivolume law library.

FOUR

A Formidable Judge

At the close of her second full term, state senator Sandra O'Connor announced that she would not seek re-election. "She was at a crossroads," a senate colleague recalled later. "She had to choose between politics and the law. She was more comfortable with the law." O'Connor, who once called law "marvelous because it is always changing," had decided to run for trial judge on the Maricopa County Superior Court. Although she had been highly successful as a legislator, she was ready to move on.

In the early 1970s, Phoenix had acquired unwelcome distinction as the nation's most crime-ridden city. O'Connor campaigned—"as a citizen, a wife, and a mother"—on the issue of law and order, promising to "help replace fear in our streets with strength

in our courtrooms." She won the 1974 election handily, defeating an incumbent judge.

A trial judge deals with opposing lawyers, presides over trials, instructs the jury (when the case involves a jury; not all do), imposes sentence in criminal cases, and generally maintains the order and efficiency of the courtroom. Judge O'Connor heard cases dealing with almost every issue that can end up in court, from murder to drug peddling to divorce.

Lawyers who appeared before O'Connor recall her as a "formidable" judge. She expected the attorneys in her courtroom to be vigorous, well-prepared representatives of their clients; she also expected them to be as hardworking and knowledgeable about the law as she was. And that, said the lawyers,

45

was asking a lot. "She frequently knew more about a case from having reviewed the file than the lawyers did," said one observer.

Phoenix lawyers agreed that O'Connor showed little tolerance for those who took the legal process lightly. "You didn't want to go in there if you weren't prepared, if you hadn't filed the papers when you were supposed to, if you hadn't researched your case properly, if you came in there on an argument without any authority and tried to snow her," said Alice Bendheim, the Phoenix attorney who had helped O'Connor revise Arizona's community-property law. "She did not appreciate having her time wasted."

Neither did she appreciate lawyers who tried to lighten the court's solemn atmosphere with humor. "You have to say something awfully funny," observed one attorney, "to get her to smile on the bench." On the other hand, recalled former public defender John Foreman, "if a lawyer was well-prepared and all business, she was pretty easy to get along with." Overall, said Foreman, he found O'Connor "fair, persuadable, and open-minded."

The Arizona judge's stern approach extended to defendants as well as their attorneys. Sometimes O'Connor even advised criminal defendants to fire their ill-prepared lawyers and hire better ones. Discussing her with a *U.S. News & World Report* writer in 1981, Arizona legislator Burton Barr said, "She's not going to coddle the criminal. Her decisions as a Superior Court judge were tough. If you have done wrong,

you are going to pay." But observers also noted O'Connor's interest in decent prison conditions. "She was known as a stiff sentencer," recalled one Phoenix attorney, "but she is also concerned about what happens to the guy once he is in the can."

One of O'Connor's most widely publicized sentences followed the trial of a former businesswoman from Scottsdale. Mother of 2 very young children and wife of a man who had abandoned her, the woman had been charged with passing $3,500 worth of bad checks. She pleaded guilty but begged O'Connor not to give her a sentence that would separate her from her children. Herself the mother of three, O'Connor surely understood the woman's pain and fear. On the other hand, it was O'Connor's job to dispense justice, not emotion. The decision proved agonizing, but O'Connor finally made it.

"You have intelligence, beauty, and two small children," she told the defendant in court. "You come from a fine and respected family. . . . Someone with all your advantages should have known better." When O'Connor read the sentence—5 to 10 years in prison—the defendant wept. "What about my babies?" she cried. O'Connor quickly left the courtroom. Alone in her chambers, she burst into tears herself. O'Connor later called the decision to jail the woman—who rejoined her children after serving 18 months in prison—the toughest she had ever made.

But O'Connor's unswerving devotion to the law produced mercy as well as

Working at the Maricopa County courthouse (above), Judge O'Connor
impressed local attorneys. She often knew more about their cases,
said the lawyers, than they did themselves.

Democrat Bruce Babbitt, Arizona's governor from 1979 to 1987, appointed O'Connor to the state Court of Appeals in 1979. He described her abilities as "astounding."

severity. In the case of a defendant named Mark Koch, for example, she canceled her own verdict when she discovered a potential miscarriage of justice. After Koch, 23, was convicted of murdering another man in a drug dispute, O'Connor sentenced him to death. When she discovered that the prosecution had withheld evidence from Koch's lawyers, however, she promptly overturned the guilty verdict and ordered a new trial.

Another murder case involved a battered woman who confessed to shooting her abusive husband. Accused of murder, the woman pleaded self-defense, but the jury returned a verdict of guilty. O'Connor, who believed the woman had indeed been defending her own life, gave her the lightest sentence possible under the law, then supported her request for a reduction of that sentence.

A third murder trial involved a man accused of burning his children to death. Although the police produced uncontestable evidence of the man's guilt, they had obtained it without obtaining a search warrant, a document required by the Constitution's Fourth Amendment. O'Connor excluded the crucial evidence from the record.

Known for her brisk efficiency, O'Connor had no patience with long-winded lawyers or anyone else who took up more court time than she considered necessary. In a mid-1980s interview with the *Washington Post*, John O'Connor illustrated his wife's crisp approach by describing a divorce case. At issue was the division of a couple's community property: 40 thoroughbred greyhounds. The opposing lawyers proposed to call witnesses to explain the merits of each of the valuable dogs—a process that might consume many days in court.

After hearing a long, involved report from the first witness, O'Connor called a halt to the canine testimony. Taking the lawyers aside, she told 1 of them to make 2 lists, each containing the names of 20 dogs and each representing the same value. When the lists were completed by one attorney, she gave them to the other and told him to select either one for his client. "In 15 minutes," John O'Connor told the *Post* reporter, "the litigation [lawsuit] was over."

In 1978, the Arizona Republican party invited Sandra O'Connor to run for governor against Democrat Bruce Babbitt. U.S. senator Barry Goldwater, a strong supporter and close friend of O'Connor's, encouraged her to make the race, and she considered the offer carefully. In the long run, however, she decided to remain on the superior court bench.

Babbitt was elected in November 1978. Eleven months later, he nominated O'Connor to fill a new vacancy on the Arizona Court of Appeals. Some political observers speculated that the governor had offered O'Connor the judgeship to head off a potentially daunting rival. Babbitt denied it. "I had to find the finest talent available," he said. "Her intellectual ability and her judgment are astounding."

As a court of appeals judge, O'Con-

nor found her work somewhat different than her job as a trial judge. Rather than presiding alone, appellate judges usually work in three-person groups. They decide broad questions of law and principle, not detailed questions of fact. Unlike trial judges, appellate judges neither conduct trials nor listen to witnesses. Instead, they hear oral arguments in which lawyers for the contending sides present their views on whatever law is in question. In a murder case, for example, a trial judge and jury will decide who pulled the trigger. But a panel of appellate court judges will rule on the subtle legal differences between manslaughter and murder or on whether the evidence used was legal.

In Arizona, the court of appeals spends one day per week listening to lawyers argue points of law. During the rest of the week, the judges read up on prior cases, statutes, and written materials submitted by the lawyers; then they write their opinions. On three-judge panels, the judges vote on the final outcome. One opinion is written for the court, but a dissenting judge, if there is one, may write a separate opinion to explain his or her differing views.

Most states have a three-tiered system of courts: trial, appellate, and supreme. These courts have *general jurisdiction*, which means they can rule on virtually any kind of controversy that may arise. The federal court system also includes three tiers, with the U.S. Supreme Court at its top. Federal courts generally hear only cases that specifically involve federal laws or

O'Connor accepts a painting, Women in Law, *for Washington, D.C.'s National Museum of Women in the Arts. The painting was presented by the National Association of Women Judges.*

cases that deal with disputes between states or citizens of different states.

The federal courts can also review and overturn state court decisions if they appear to run counter to federal constitutional provisions. This most often occurs in criminal matters. If a state court, for example, sentences a murderer to death, a federal court may review the case to ensure that the proceedings and sentence are consistent with the requirements of the U.S. Constitution.

During her 18-month tenure on the appeals court, O'Connor published 29 opinions, most of them dealing with such routine issues as workers' compensation, landlord-tenant disputes, and criminal matters. While she was an appeals judge, predictably enough, O'Connor continued to work as an organizer and volunteer. She also served on the boards of Blue Cross/Blue Shield and the Phoenix Historical Society. She became a trustee of Stanford University. She was a member of the National Association of Women Judges, and in 1980 she organized an association of woman lawyers in Arizona.

Both as a trial judge and as a state appellate judge, O'Connor earned high ratings from the Arizona State Bar Association. The evaluations, based on a poll of Arizona lawyers, gave her top scores for thoroughness and meticulously written opinions. They rated her somewhat lower, however, on her personal dealings with attorneys, some of whom objected to her no-nonsense, get-on-with-business approach. But it was

Family members surround O'Connor after her 1981 Supreme Court nomination. At rear are the nominee's husband and sons: John, Jay, Brian, and Scott O'Connor.

Ronald Reagan chats with O'Connor in the White House Rose Garden. The president called his Supreme Court nominee "truly a person for all seasons."

not a style she planned to change. O'Connor would continue to expect as much from others as she did of herself.

O'Connor's experience as a judge, first at the trial level, then on the appeals court, marked another chapter of her education in public service. In seven years on the bench, she gained a deep understanding of the complex relationship between state and federal courts. Perhaps because she entered the nation's judicial network at what might be called its bottom corner—at the level of a state trial judge—O'Connor has always championed the lower courts. Federal courts, she has asserted, should review lower-court decisions less frequently than they do.

In a 1981 article in the *William and Mary Law Review*, O'Connor aired some of her views. State appellate judges, she wrote, "occasionally become so frustrated with the extent of federal court intervention that they simply abdicate [withdraw] in favor of the federal jurisdiction." Noting that the United States "appears to be the only major country with two parallel court systems," O'Connor urged federal judges to exercise more caution and show more deference to their state court colleagues. It was a viewpoint that she would take with her to her next place of employment, Washington, D.C.

For most lawyers, a state appellate judgeship is the pinnacle of a successful career. O'Connor herself did not expect a great deal more. "I anticipated that I would live the balance of my life in our adobe house on the desert," she said in the early 1980s, "where my husband and I had many friends, a pleasant way of life, and where we expected our sons to settle." But Sandra Day O'Connor had spent a lifetime doing more than she or anyone else expected. On July 7, 1981, President Ronald Reagan announced her appointment to the Supreme Court.

O'Connor fields reporters' questions during a July 1981 interview. Despite relentless press grilling, the judge remained discreetly silent on many issues.

FIVE

"Abigail Adams Would Be Pleased"

Sandra O'Connor "is far from a shrinking violet," said a former colleague on the Arizona Court of Appeals. Talking to a reporter in 1981, Judge Donald Froeb added, "She always assumes the leadership role." Unshrinking or not, O'Connor must sometimes have longed for invisibility in the days that followed her Supreme Court nomination. Strangers accosted her on the street, asking if she knew how much she resembled Sandra Day O'Connor. Others waved autograph books at her or insisted on shaking her hand. Some people would look her over, then whisper to friends, "It doesn't look like her, but it's her." Photographers and reporters followed her in droves.

The Supreme Court's first female nominee had become America's woman of the hour. O'Connor's fellow citizens—few of whom had ever heard of her until her nomination to the Court—were suddenly fascinated by this 51-year-old Arizonan. To satisfy their readers' curiosity, reporters asked O'Connor endless personal questions about her children, her husband, her parents, her hobbies, her home. And, of course, they asked for her views on abortion and other major issues of the day.

The Arizona judge responded to press questions with her customary aplomb, but she revealed little about her views on political or social matters. As she was expected to do, she released an account of her own and her husband's financial assets: The O'Connors' combined assets totaled just under $1.2 million, some of it in stocks, some in a share of the Lazy B and other properties, and the rest in the couple's investment in John O'Connor's law firm, by then one of the largest and most successful in the Southwest.

On other matters, however, Sandra O'Connor maintained a cool reserve, even during her September 1981 interrogation by the all-male Senate Judiciary Committee. Reporting to the Senate Office Building for her three-day confirmation hearings, O'Connor was escorted by her husband and sons. She made an opening statement, which included an impassioned paragraph about the importance of marriage, then settled down to answer queries from committee members.

As antiabortion demonstrators marched outside the Senate Office Building, senators cross-examined O'Connor about her position on the subject. They concentrated on several votes she had cast as an Arizona legislator: In 1970, for example, she had supported the repeal of an Arizona law that made abortion a criminal act. (The repeal effort had failed, and the law remained on the state's books.) Did O'Connor's 1970 vote, asked the U.S.

O'Connor's husband and son watch intently as she makes a point during her confirmation hearings. Repeatedly asked about her views on abortion, she finally said she "opposed" it.

senators, mean that she favored the legalization of abortion?

After explaining that she had considered the Arizona law too vague, O'Connor said, "At that time I believed some change was appropriate." She said her opinion had changed over the years and that she would no longer favor repeal of the antiabortion statute. O'Connor then emphasized two other votes she had cast in the 1970s, one for limiting the use of state funds to pay for abortions for poor women, the other allowing hospital employees to refuse to assist in abortions.

Committee members asked O'Connor whether, as a Supreme Court justice, she would work toward reversing *Roe v. Wade*, the 1973 Court ruling that had eliminated most abortion restrictions. The nominee said that she could not predict her response to future cases and that she did not believe her personal opinions would affect her work on the Court. However, she conceded, "My own view is that I am opposed to abortion either as birth control or otherwise." Then she added philosophically, "I'm over the hill. I'm not going to be pregnant anymore, so perhaps it is easy for me to draw such a strict line."

O'Connor went on to say that she felt the whole abortion question was better asked of lawmakers than of judges. "I know well the difference between a legislator and a judge," she said, "and the role of the judge is to interpret the law, not make it"—a statement that clearly impressed some of the committee's legislators.

A clearly impatient Senator Jeremiah Denton listens to O'Connor parry a question about abortion. In the end, the Alabama Republican abstained from voting on the nominee.

Led by Dr. Carl McIntire (right), president of the International Council of Christian Churches, a group of antiabortion demonstrators marches on Capitol Hill.

No matter how many times she was asked to take a stand on the legality of abortion, O'Connor politely refused, insisting she could not discuss matters that might come before the Supreme Court. One senator, Republican Jeremiah Denton of Alabama, appeared slightly exasperated after questioning O'Connor about abortion for 30 minutes. When the committee chairman asked Denton if he would like to have another 15 minutes of question time, the plainly frustrated senator said, "I don't know whether another *month* would do."

The subject of the Equal Rights Amendment came up toward the end of the hearings. If she became a Supreme Court justice, O'Connor was asked, would she support the next campaign to pass the ERA? She said no; she believed that such political action would be "inappropriate" for a member of the Court. At this point, Democratic senator Joseph Biden of Delaware said he believed O'Connor should become "more than just another justice." He continued, "I just don't want you to wall yourself off. You have an obligation to be an advocate for women." Spectators broke into loud applause, but O'Connor remained serenely silent.

In its report on the three-day hearing, *Newsweek* magazine said that O'Connor "clung carefully to three rules of conduct for a successful justice-to-be: It's better to be seen than heard, speak only when spoken to, and try not to discuss religion or politics."

Senate approval of a Supreme Court nominee is by no means assured. Two candidates for the bench, Judge G. Harrold Carswell of Florida and Judge Clement F. Haynsworth of South Carolina, had recently been rejected despite their endorsement by then president Richard Nixon. O'Connor's approval, however, appeared close to inevitable. Her supporters included Democrats, Republicans, and feminists of both sexes and all political persuasions. Other women demonstrated special enthusiasm for the nominee. In fact, observed syndicated columnist Mary McGrory, "if anything happened to O'Connor on her way to the Supreme Court, the women of America would storm the Senate Judiciary Committee and trash it."

The Senate committee voted, 17–0, to confirm O'Connor. (Only one member, Jeremiah Denton, failed to vote aye; he cast no vote at all.) A week after the hearings, the full Senate confirmed O'Connor's appointment by a vote of 99–0. The United States had finally placed a woman on the Supreme Court. The move, commented *Time* magazine, "provided not only a breakthrough on the bench but a powerful push forward in the shamefully long and needlessly tortuous march of women toward full equality in American society."

After the Senate's approving vote, Vice-president George Bush and a crowd of cheering supporters greeted O'Connor on the Capitol steps. Gesturing toward the nearby Supreme Court

Justice O'Connor greets supporters after her confirmation. With her are (left to right) Attorney General William French Smith, Senator Barry Goldwater, Vice-president George Bush, and Senator Strom Thurmond.

Chief Justice Warren Burger swears in the Supreme Court's first female justice. Holding two family Bibles, John O'Connor assists in the historic ceremony.

building, the beaming Arizonan said, "My hope is that 10 years from now, after I've been across the street at work for a while, they'll all be glad they gave me that wonderful vote."

Later that day O'Connor spoke at a celebratory banquet. "Thomas Jefferson and James Madison would be turning over in their graves right now," she said with a smile, "but let's hope Abigail Adams would be pleased." (Adams, wife of the second U.S. president, had been an early and ardent champion of women's rights.)

On the morning of Monday, September 28, Justice Sandra Day O'Connor went to work at her new office, the vast, marble-columned Supreme Court building on Washington's First Street. The Court's new term would open a week later—on Monday, October 5. (The Court traditionally starts its annual term on the first Monday in October, then stays in session until it announces the year's final decision, usually the following June. After that, the Court goes into recess until the next October.)

Awaiting O'Connor and her fellow justices in 1981 were more than 1,000 petitions from litigants who wanted the Supreme Court to review their cases. In the week to come, the Court's nine justices would hold secret conferences to discuss these cases and to decide which ones they would accept for review. Of the approximately 5,000 requests it receives each year, the Court generally hears only about 150. In cases that are not selected for review, the decision of the lower court, state or federal, is simply left undisturbed.

Because the Court makes its views known through the cases it decides, a justice's first task is to choose cases wisely. "It takes considerable time," O'Connor has said, "before one feels generally familiar with the contexts in which the petitioners come to the Court." Intelligent selection of cases, she asserts, requires an understanding of "the extent to which a Supreme Court ruling on the issue is really needed, and whether the particular facts and legal posture of the case present a proper vehicle for deciding the issue."

The justices vote—as they do in all matters that they decide—on which cases they will accept. Each justice, the chief justice included, has one vote. In other situations the majority rules, but by Court tradition, four votes are enough to bring a case to the Court for final disposition. The conference meetings, a tradition in themselves, are held in a large room next to the chief justice's chamber. Like almost every room in the courthouse, the conference room is lined with legal books. At its center stands a huge, highly polished table.

As the Court's junior (most recently appointed) justice in 1981, O'Connor was given the seat nearest the conference room door—another long-standing Court tradition. No one but the justices may enter the room during a conference; the junior justice is responsible for receiving and passing out messages. He or she also records the votes and takes notes on the deliberations. (O'Connor is no longer the junior justice; in 1986, that honor went to Justice Antonin Scalia, and in 1989 to Justice Anthony Kennedy.)

After the justices select the cases they will review, the parties are notified, and a date is set for written and oral argument by the opposing attorneys. These attorneys then file voluminous documents—ironically called *briefs*—with the Court. The justices and their clerks study these papers carefully. Frequently, organizations and individuals who are not directly involved in the case will file *amicus curiae* (friend of the court) briefs in support of one side or the other. The justices will study these, too.

Oral arguments are presented to the justices in the courtroom, which is open to the public. During 2 weeks of most months between October and May, the justices hear 4 oral arguments each day; each side is ordinarily allowed 30 minutes to present its case. After the conclusion of the arguments, the justices meet for a *case conference*, a session at which they discuss the case and take a vote.

Accompanied by her new boss, Associate Justice Sandra Day O'Connor models her professional garb on the steps of the Supreme Court building.

Proudly flanking a newly minted justice are (from the left) Harry Day, John O'Connor, Ada Mae Day, Chief Justice Burger, and Brian, Jay, and Scott O'Connor.

The justices' decisions, of course, are based on more than the arguments they have just heard. To reach their verdicts, they draw on the briefs they have read and on the testimony and information already presented to the lower courts. The justices also rely on their knowledge of constitutional law and of *precedents*, earlier Court rulings that may affect the current case.

After the justices have reached a decision, one of them writes a majority opinion. If the chief justice is a member of the majority, he either writes the opinion himself or assigns it to another majority voter. When the chief has voted with the minority, the opinion is written or assigned by the senior justice in the majority.

Other justices, meanwhile, may—and often do—write separate opinions. Such an opinion may be a *concurrence*, in which a justice agrees with the majority but adds his or her own special thoughts on the matter. It may also be a *dissent*, in which a minority justice explains why he or she disagrees with the majority opinion.

Writing opinions is a justice's single most important task. Opinions demonstrate to the parties, winners and losers alike, that their case has been heard, carefully considered, and thoughtfully resolved. More important, opinions set out the legal system's definitive pronouncements on issues of law, making them clear to other courts, to the other branches of government, to the legal profession, to the press, and to the public. Each term of the Court pro-

O'Connor believed her appointment to the Court would have pleased one of her heroines, Abigail Adams (above). The nation's second first lady, Adams was also among its first feminists.

Equipment in the Court's Information Office includes a relatively modern word processor. Steadfastly traditional, the Court is slow to alter its routines and practices.

duces some 5,000 pages of opinions and rulings.

Until these opinions are published, they are a matter of great secrecy. After an opinion is announced, the Court clerk distributes printed copies. If the case is an important one, the release will be followed by a wild scramble:

Lawyers will rush to notify their clients, reporters to file stories for that evening's television news or the next day's newspaper headlines. Spring is usually a time of frantic activity inside and around the Court.

Through the years, the Court has issued only a few dozen printed copies of each opinion, often not enough for all the individuals and groups with an interest in a particular case. Early 1990, however, brought a change: The Court announced that, beginning with the spring term of that year, it would electronically transmit full texts of all rulings around the nation. The move was applauded by news and legal organizations.

The American Bar Association noted that the Court's new computerized transmission service would, for the first time, make Supreme Court opinions immediately "available for the average guy." The nation, added the *New York Times* approvingly, had entered "the age of a more user-friendly Court."

O'Connor raised a few judicial eyebrows when she started an exercise class for female Court employees. "I'm more productive when I feel good physically," she explained.

SIX

"She's Just What She Is"

Each of the Supreme Court's nine justices occupies a suite of rooms ("chambers") in the vast marble courthouse. Sandra Day O'Connor's chambers are on the second floor, at the northwest corner of the Court building. Her private office, an imposing room with a 15-foot ceiling and carved wood paneling, contains a massive desk, several comfortable couches and chairs, and rows of shelves crowded with legal books. Scattered around the area are family pictures, Native American art from Arizona, plants, and mementos from friends.

Next to O'Connor's private office is a middle room housing a messenger and two secretaries who handle the justice's voluminous mail, maintain her calendar, and supervise the endless flow of paper into and out of her cham-

bers. The next room is occupied by O'Connor's four law clerks, young attorneys just two years out of law school. Typically, these aides will have clerked on a court of appeals the year before and are now spending one intense, exhilarating year working closely with the justice. It is the job of the law clerks to write summaries of the thousands of petitions requesting Supreme Court review of lower-court cases. The law clerks also prepare "bench memos" for the justice on the cases that have been accepted for argument and help her prepare her final opinions.

On a typical day during the Court's October-to-June term, Justice O'Connor leaves her house at about 7:30 in the morning, sometimes driving to work with her husband. When she arrives at the courthouse, she attends the exercise class she established when she first joined the Court. Attired in black leotards, she and several other women of the Court spend 40 minutes practicing aerobics.

"I think physical fitness is enormously important to your capacity to do mental-fitness work," O'Connor told an interviewer in 1985. "I'm more productive with my work when I feel good physically." O'Connor's exercise classes gained quick acceptance among the Court's female employees, but they caused a few raised eyebrows among the males. One fellow justice reportedly said, "It took some getting used to, seeing those black-leotarded ladies in the halls of the Court."

Her workout finished by 8:45, O'Connor settles down to work in her chambers. She often begins her day by studying petitions for review. Like her colleagues, O'Connor looks for cases that present far-reaching but unexplored points of law. One case, for example, might indicate a major conflict among the federal courts of appeal—perhaps on an obscure but important question of federal banking law or environmental protection. Another might present an important question of individual rights and freedoms, perhaps involving the press's right to publish secret government papers. Or a case could suggest a serious conflict between two branches of the federal government, as when Congress claims the right to overrule a decision by a government agency through the vote of the House or Senate alone. Most of the

Justices of the Supreme Court sit for a portrait in 1988. Seated are (left to right) Thurgood Marshall, William Brennan, Chief Justice William Rehnquist, Byron White, and Harry Blackmun. At rear are: Antonin Scalia, John Paul Stevens III, Sandra Day O'Connor, and Anthony M. Kennedy.

5,000 petitions filed with the Court each year raise no such questions. Those that do often make history.

Although it occupies a relatively small part of a justice's time, the oral argument is the most public of his or her activities. On argument days—Mondays, Tuesdays, and Wednesdays for about two weeks of each month of the Court's term—O'Connor joins her fellow justices in the conference room at exactly 9:55 A.M. The colleagues then exchange handshakes, a symbolic ritual that suggests cordiality despite the major differences of opinion that may separate the participants.

At 10:00, the nine black-robed justices line up behind a red velvet curtain; each stands directly in back of the tall leather chair he or she will occupy at the Court's great mahogany bench. After the Court clerk says, "All rise,"

The reading room of the Supreme Court library provides its users with a tranquil but magnificent place to study.

the justices simultaneously enter the room and take their place. The chief justice sits at the center; the seats of the other justices are determined by seniority. To the chief justice's right sits the justice who has served longest on the Court; to his left sits the justice with the next highest seniority. The remaining justices sit in an alternating pattern of seniority; the junior justice sits at the far left and the second most junior justice at the far right.

Oral arguments offer spectators a sense of high drama. The setting itself is impressive: framed by 24 marble columns that rise 44 feet to meet a sculpted marble panel, the vast courtroom reminds some observers of a great cathedral. A session begins with a command from the marshal of the Court: "All rise!" At that point, lawyers, press, and spectators stand, and the justices step from behind the curtains to take their place at the bench. "Oyez, oyez, oyez," the marshal intones solemnly. (*Oyez*, a corruption of "hear ye," is pronounced OH-yay.) "All persons having business before the honorable, the Supreme Court of the United States, are admonished to draw near and give their attention, for the Court is now sitting. God save the United States and this Honorable Court."

After justices and audience take their seat, oral argument begins. Obeying a nod and a brief word from Chief Justice William H. Rehnquist, the first lawyer moves to the podium before the bench. "Chief Justice Rehnquist, and may it please the Court," is the standard opening line. Lawyers are usually allowed

A row of leather chairs await their occupants—the nine justices of the Supreme Court—in the deserted courtroom. The Court permits no interior photography when it is in session.

about half an hour to present their case, but in most instances, the presentation is steered more by the justices than by the lawyers. The justices, of course, have already read the legal briefs, and they know the facts of the case. This is a time for lawyers to answer the Court's questions and to pursue new lines of argument. When the first lawyer finishes, the opposing lawyer steps up to undergo a similar interrogation from the bench.

On oral argument days, two cases are presented in the morning, another two in the afternoon. Spectators leave the Court with their own guesses about what the justices are thinking and how they will vote. Reporters search for clues in the questions that a justice asked or did not ask each side. Because she is in the Court's political center, O'Connor's views are often the subject of great speculation. This is especially true in the closest cases, where her "swing" vote may decide the Court's final ruling.

O'Connor is known for asking hard questions and expecting thoughtful, well-informed answers. Giving her a political label, however, has proved difficult. A loyal Republican, she is regarded as generally conservative, but not, as one observer commented, "out of the knee-jerk mold." The *New York Times* described her as "a sometime conservative with a moderate, even progressive streak. [She is] a determined woman but not a dogmatic [inflexible] one." And an attorney who knew her well in Arizona called her "no more liberal than the man in the moon." She is, he said, "conservative to moderate." Another colleague called O'Connor "not liberal or conservative—she's just what she is."

After oral arguments and the conference vote, the justices draft and circulate their opinions among themselves. Most of the interchange between the justices at this stage is in writing. A justice may join an opinion outright or

ask for changes, major or minor, before signing on. Occasionally, a justice will change sides, persuaded by the eloquent opinion of the other side. When this happens in a case where the vote had been 5–4, the dissenters may suddenly find themselves in the majority.

In a typical term, O'Connor may be the author of 16 majority opinions and a similar number of concurrences or dissents. The majority ("for the Court") opinions will usually be the longest, occasionally running to as many as 50 printed pages. Like the other justices, O'Connor will state her understanding of the facts of the case, note the legal principles involved, and explain the reasoning she employed to arrive at her decision.

Supreme Court opinions are published in a series of volumes called the *United States Reports*. In O'Connor's case, the rulings are prefaced by the sentence, "Justice O'Connor delivered the opinion of the Court." These words reflect a bit of history. Until recently, members of the Court were always known individually as "Mr. Justice" and collectively as "the brethren." Apparently aware that a woman would join the Court sooner or later, officials quietly dropped the *Mr.* some years before O'Connor's appointment. Perhaps no one wanted to argue about such alternate titles as "Mrs. Justice" or "Ms. Justice" or even "Madam Justice." In any event, the proper title today is simply "Justice O'Connor" or "Justice Kennedy."

O'Connor and her staff usually work six days a week. Meeting with one or more of her clerks each day, the justice may discuss a case that is about to be argued or an opinion that needs to be written. Several times each week, O'Connor gathers all four clerks together to discuss the Court's next "sitting," or scheduled series of oral arguments. While the pace is intense, the O'Connor chambers are reportedly a cheerful place to work. The justice and the clerks often pass around popcorn, joking and laughing even as they discuss the most complex and obscure points of law. The work in the O'Connor chambers is always serious, but the atmosphere is rarely solemn.

On Saturdays when she works, O'Connor often brings a lunch of Mexican food to share with everyone in her chambers. Each year, she organizes several office outings, taking her staff to the National Arboretum, the Folger Library, or the Smithsonian Institution. O'Connor remembers the birthday of each of her clerks with a cake and a short office party. She knows that when people work 60 or 70 hours a week, as they usually do in her chambers, occasional breaks are essential.

Another O'Connor tradition is the annual staff "adventure." One year, the justice took her clerks white-water raft-

Court exhibits include the last edition of the United States Reports *printed by the antiquated hot-metal typesetting process. The Court finally switched to computer typesetting in 1981.*

ing on Pennsylvania's challenging Youghiogheny River. Before the group started down the river, their guide emphasized an important rule of rafting: No one leaves the craft, not even if a member of the party is swept overboard. (Properly equipped rafters wear life jackets; if they land in the water, they put their legs straight out and steer themselves to a place where their companions can retrieve them.) On this particular trip, however, everybody for-

O'Connor hosts a 1989 garden party for a group of her former law clerks and their children, affectionately dubbed "grandclerks" by the Supreme Court associate justice.

got the rules. Sandra O'Connor herself was swept overboard. Without a moment's hesitation, her clerks jumped into the river after her.

As it turned out, O'Connor saved herself with little effort. The clerks, however, received a tongue-lashing from the raft guide, furious that his instructions had been so thoroughly disobeyed. Even so, said one of the would-be rescuers later, "if you are clerking for Sandra O'Connor, you aren't going to be the one to let her drown. Her other clerks, and a few million other people besides, would never forgive you!"

Her aides' intense loyalty springs in part from O'Connor's concern for them. One former O'Connor clerk recalled that he had often worked in her chambers until very late at night. After a violent crime had occurred in the neighborhood, O'Connor made special arrangements with the Court security officers: The clerk could now bring his golden retriever into the building at night so that he could walk home for dinner and then safely return for several more hours of work. "My dog," said the clerk, "spent more evening hours gazing at the U.S. Reports than most students do in law school."

Justice O'Connor, continued her former aide, "maintains a high pace of activity, demands tireless work, and expects the highest quality from everyone around her. But she gives as much from herself, and by setting the example gets as much back from everyone who works for her. Being a Supreme Court justice, or working with one, is surely one of the most challenging and interesting jobs in the country. And no more so than in Justice O'Connor's chambers."

Every year, O'Connor hosts a dinner party for her current and former clerks. (Traditionally, a Supreme Court justice employs four clerks, each of whom serves for one year.) Also invited to an annual party are the children, or "grandclerks," of O'Connor's aides. Young lawyers who learn the intricate ways of the Court under O'Connor's tutelage go on to practice with major law firms, teach at prominent law schools around the nation, or even become judges themselves. In the fall of 1989, O'Connor had the pleasure of taking part in a very special ceremony: She swore in one of her former clerks, Ruth MacGregor, as a judge on the same Arizona court of appeals bench she had once occupied herself.

Working for a Supreme Court justice teaches more than Court procedures and fine points of constitutional law. O'Connor's clerks, like those of the other eight justices, inevitably acquire a sense of their boss's attitudes and personal philosophy. O'Connor's passionate devotion to the Constitution, for example, cannot help but transmit itself to the people who work closely with her.

An interviewer recently asked O'Connor an important question: "What should young people know about the Constitution by the time they complete high school?" Her response revealed the intensity of her feeling for America's system of govern-

ment. "Our Constitution," she said, "was not intended solely, or even primarily, for judges. The strength of our . . . freedoms depends on how firmly they stand in the hearts of our citizens.

"One of the most respected judges in this century, Learned Hand," she continued, "understood this very well. He explained: 'Liberty lies in the hearts of men and women; when it dies there, no constitution, no law, no court can save it; no constitution, no court, no law can even do much to help it. While it lies there, it needs no constitution, no law, no court to save it.' "

Warming to her theme, O'Connor continued, "But our understanding today must go beyond the recognition that 'liberty lies in [our] hearts' to the further recognition that only citizens with knowledge about the content and meaning of our constitutional guarantees of liberty are likely to cherish these concepts. Such knowledge is not passed down from generation to generation through the gene pool; it must be learned anew by each generation.

"Without an educational structure which fosters and encourages each successive group of students to learn about the structure of our government and the history of its development," she explained, "we would soon see young hearts barren of those sentiments and understandings out of which our nation came into existence. To fulfill our obligations as citizens, to understand and uphold our Constitution, we must have educational institutions which foster the acceptance of the individual responsibility of citizenship."

O'Connor, America's first female Supreme Court justice, meets Margaret Thatcher, Britain's first female prime minister, during a 1984 visit to London.

SEVEN

"The Justice Holds the Key"

Becoming a justice of the United States Supreme Court is an extraordinary achievement for any American. No other national office, except for the presidency, confers equal power and significance. The Court is the highest tribunal in the country, the court of final appeal, and the ultimate authority on questions of federal law. It is the only court explicitly established by the U.S. Constitution, which states in Article III: "The judicial Power of the United States, shall be vested in one supreme Court, and in such inferior Courts as the Congress may from time to time ordain and establish."

But despite its vital importance to Americans of both sexes and all races, the Supreme Court remained a solid bastion of white male power for 178 years. No nonwhite ascended to the Court's great bench until 1967, when black civil rights leader Thurgood Marshall became the Supreme Court's 96th justice. Marshall's appointment came 110 years after Supreme Court chief justice Roger Taney, ruling on the case of former slave Dred Scott, declared that blacks were property, not citizens.

It took women even longer than blacks to find a place on the Supreme Court. Sandra Day O'Connor's rise to the bench came 108 years after Supreme Court justice Joseph P. Bradley denied Myra Bradwell's plea to become a lawyer. According to Justice Bradley, the practice of law required the "decision and firmness which are presumed to predominate in the sterner [male] sex."

For nearly a century after the *Bradwell* case, the Supreme Court continued to support laws that discriminated against women. It upheld Missouri's male-only voting laws and a West Virginia law that restricted jury service to men. Asserting that a woman "looks to her brother and depends on him," the Court approved an Oregon law that "protected" women by forbidding them to work long hours, at night, or in hazardous occupations. In 1948, the Court found no constitutional violation in a Michigan law that prohibited

The Court sits for a portrait in 1926. Until the appointments of Thurgood Marshall and Sandra O'Connor, justices were white, male, and usually middle-aged and wealthy.

most women from being bartenders. As recently as 1961, the Court upheld a Florida law requiring women to serve on juries only if they volunteered. A woman's place, the Court reasoned in this case, was at the "center of home and family life."

But by the 1970s, the Supreme Court was ready to overturn some laws that treated women and men unequally. In a series of opinions beginning in 1971, the Court began to reject the notion that women were unfit to be lawyers, bartenders, or astronauts. Gradually, the Court built up the principle that sex-based classifications are to be scrutinized with special care. Classifications are not always invalid, but the Court became increasingly suspicious of those that seem to be based on "romantic paternalism" or other outdated, gender-based notions.

First, the Court struck down an Idaho law that gave men automatic preference over women in handling estates. Next came a ruling that married women in the armed forces are entitled to the same benefits as married men. In 1975, the Supreme Court invalidated a Utah law that required parents to support their sons until the age of 21 but their daughters only until the age of 18. (That law was based on the antiquated idea that young men needed to study, whereas young women would either marry or take unskilled work.) Also in 1975, the Court ruled that widowers were entitled to the same Social Security survivors' benefits as widows. The following year, the Court struck down an Oklahoma law that allowed women

Former civil rights activist Thurgood Marshall, the Court's 96th justice, is its first—and to date, only—black member. Marshall joined the Court in 1967.

81

Tootsie Bess tends bar at her café in Nashville, Tennessee. Until the mid-20th century, the laws of many states excluded women from such "men's work."

to buy beer at 18 but required men to wait until the age of 21.

Some of these decisions were based on the Constitution's Fourteenth Amendment, which guarantees "the equal protection of the laws" to all citizens. Other rulings came under the Civil Rights Act of 1964, a federal law that (among other things) prohibits sex-based discrimination in the workplace. A 1978 ruling, for example, declared that women may not be required to contribute more into their pension plans than men, even though women, who generally live longer than men, will (on average) collect more from these programs than men. And a 1977 Court decision held that employers may not deprive women of certain types of job seniority if they take maternity leave.

Case by case, a new constitutional principle emerged: State and federal governments may not discriminate against anyone solely because of sex, much as they may not discriminate solely because of race. This principle was already fairly well established by the time Sandra O'Connor joined the Court. When she was appointed in 1981, O'Connor became living proof that the legal profession, at least, was finally and definitely open to all.

In law, once a principle has been established, it applies equally to all. Thus, if it is illegal to discriminate on the basis of sex, it is illegal whether the discrimination hurts women or hurts men. A good example of this principle can be seen in the case of Joe Hogan,

Leading the pack, astronauts Kathryn Sullivan (left) and Sally Ride prepare for a space mission in 1984. By this point, women had entered almost every professional field.

Sandra Day O'Connor's first major test as a Supreme Court justice. In 1979, 106 years after Myra Bradwell lost her bid to become a lawyer, Joe Hogan resolved to get a bachelor's degree in nursing. Already a registered nurse, Hogan had worked for five years as a nursing supervisor in a Columbus, Mississippi, medical center; the extra degree would allow him to earn a higher salary and make him eligible for specialized training.

Hogan applied to the nursing school of the Mississippi University for Women in his hometown of Columbus.

Founded in 1884, the state-supported school had always limited its enrollment to women; it rejected Hogan on the basis of his sex. Asserting that the university's action had violated the Constitution's equal protection guarantee, Hogan sued. His case moved through a federal trial court, then through a federal court of appeals, and finally to the U.S. Supreme Court, where it was argued in March 1982. For the first time in history, an important sex discrimination case was heard by a Supreme Court whose justices included a woman.

On July 1, 1982, the Court handed down its decision, written by Justice Sandra O'Connor. A state, she said, may not constitutionally "exclude or 'protect' members of one gender because they are presumed to suffer from an inherent handicap or to be innately inferior." In some rare situations, she observed, classifications based on gender might be justified, but only if they plainly served "important governmental objectives"—clearly not the case at the Mississippi nursing school.

No law that treats the sexes differently, added O'Connor, may reflect "archaic and stereotypic notions"; excluding males from the nursing school "tends to perpetuate the stereotyped view of nursing as an exclusively women's job." In cases relating to sex discrimination, said O'Connor, the courts should use "reasoned analysis" rather than automatically applying "traditional, often inaccurate, assumptions about the proper roles of men and women." Finally, in a footnote to her opinion, O'Connor referred to the Court's May 1873 ruling on Myra Bradwell, making the point that, in most circumstances, gender-based discrimination was history.

O'Connor's views on gender cases are, of course, of special interest and influence. But the Supreme Court's agenda is filled with variety; the issues change constantly and reach all areas of American life. Like those of her colleagues, O'Connor's opinions span the entire range. In her first term on the Court—1981–82—the 152 cases accepted for review dealt with such issues as the death penalty, school libraries, busing to achieve school integration, pornography, and affirmative action (a program designed to correct long-term racial imbalances in schools and workplaces).

Among O'Connor's first written opinions was *Rose v. Lundy*. In this case, a man named Lundy sued for release from a state prison, claiming that his constitutional rights had been violated during his trial. The issue gave O'Connor the opportunity to reemphasize her faith in the state court system. Writing for the Court's 8–1 majority, she ruled that Lundy had not fully explored the remedies available to him in the state courts. This concept, called the "total exhaustion" rule, holds that an individual should use up, or "exhaust," all possibilities available in the lower courts before bringing a case to the Supreme Court.

In two subsequent opinions, *Engle v. Isaac* and *U.S. v. Frady*, O'Connor continued to favor restricting the rights of prisoners to obtain new trials. These decisions, observed an O'Connor biographer, Judith Bentley, "were part of a conservative trend by the Court to back the arguments of the police, prosecutors, and state judges and reject those of defendants."

At one time or another, almost everyone is touched by Supreme Court decisions. Individual decisions may seem narrow, directed at only one specific set of facts, but as time passes, these decisions come together to become a set of principles. Illustrating this process are the Court decisions

Mississippi University for Women (above) admitted no men from its founding in 1884 until 1982, when Justice O'Connor ordered it to accept a qualified male nursing student.

that have affected schools and students. In 1954, for example, *Brown v. Board of Education of Topeka* demolished the basis for legal segregation in American public schools. This landmark case, brought by future Supreme Court associate justice Thurgood Marshall, affected millions of American children by forcing the nation to start integrating its public educational facilities.

Supreme Court decisions have touched schools and their students in many other ways as well. Indeed,

school cases have dealt with free speech, personal privacy, free exercise of religion, and other national issues. In 1982, for example, the Court voted 5–4 to limit the freedom of public school officials to remove allegedly offensive books from their libraries.

The case began when a Long Island, New York, school board, acting on the demands of a group of parents, removed nine books from the school library. Outraged by the loss of such popular modern works as Kurt Vonnegut's

Nettie Hunt tells her three-year-old daughter, Nikie, about the historic May 1954 Supreme Court decision that outlawed racial segregation in American public schools.

Slaughterhouse Five, Eldridge Cleaver's *Soul on Ice*, Oliver La Farge's *Laughing Boy*, and Richard Wright's *Black Boy*, students at the Island Trees Union Free School sued the board.

The students won, but O'Connor wrote an emphatic dissent to her colleagues' opinion. "If the school board can set the curriculum, select teachers, and determine initially what books to purchase for the school library," she wrote, "it surely can decide which books to discontinue or remove from the school library so long as it does not also interfere with the right of students to read the material and to discuss it."

Another school case began in Hazelwood, Missouri, in 1983. Asserting that student-newspaper articles about divorce and student pregnancy were inappropriate, a local high school principal deleted two pages of the newspaper. Student editors of the paper, which was published as part of the school's journalism program, sued. When the case went to the Supreme Court in 1988, O'Connor joined the majority in ruling against the students. Public school officials, she wrote, have broad power to censor school publications, plays, and other "school-sponsored expressive activities."

Among the issues that return to the Court repeatedly is the overlap of religion and public schools. In 1968, the Court struck down an Arkansas law that forbade the teaching of evolution in public schools and state colleges. The law, ruled the Court, violated the Constitution's First Amendment guarantee of freedom of religion. Citing freedom of religion again in 1980, the Court invalidated a Kentucky law that required the posting of the Ten Commandments in each public school classroom. When she joined the Court in 1981, O'Connor had to ponder these earlier decisions and decide where she stood on the issues they raised.

O'Connor's position gradually became clear. At issue in a 1983 case, *Lynch v. Donnelly*, was the right of a city to erect a publicly owned religious display (in this case, a Christmas nativity scene). Lower courts had ruled that the nativity scene, displayed in Pawtucket, Rhode Island, violated the Constitution's First Amendment by explicitly endorsing an exclusively Christian symbol.

But Chief Justice Warren Burger, writing for the Court majority, pointed out that the Pawtucket display included many nonreligious figures, including a Santa Claus house, candy-striped poles, and figures of carolers. Its basic purpose, he said, was to express "a friendly community spirit of good will in keeping with the season." Four justices—Brennan, Marshall, Blackmun, and Stevens—emphatically disagreed with Burger. The nativity scene's "effect on minority religious groups, as well as on those who may reject all religion," they said, "is to convey the message that their views are not similarly worthy of public recognition nor entitled to public support."

O'Connor joined Burger. In her separate concurring opinion, she wrote that the nativity scene "does not communi-

Dearborn, Michigan's city hall marks Christmas with a nativity scene. In 1983, with O'Connor concurring, the Court approved certain publicly sponsored religious displays.

cate a message that the government intends to endorse . . . Christian beliefs." The display, she said, "celebrates a public holiday, and no one contends that declaration of that holiday is understood to be an endorsement of religion."

The Pawtucket nativity decision, observed the *New York Times*, "was the Supreme Court's most important ruling in some years on the permissible boundary between government and organized religion. It significantly shifted the boundary in favor of religion."

In 1985, O'Connor concurred in the Court's 6–3 ruling against an Alabama law that permitted a daily 1-minute period of silent meditation or prayer in public schools. The Court's opinion reinforced its previously stated principle that "government must pursue a course of complete neutrality toward religion," neither encouraging nor discouraging it. In the same year, 1985, the Court agreed to review a Connecticut law that gave employees the right not to work on their own sabbath.

The Connecticut case, *Thornton v. Caldor*, began when a Caldor department store manager, Donald E. Thornton, told his employer that his religion forbade him to work on Sundays. The store responded by demoting him to a clerical job, and he sued, citing the sabbath law. After Thornton won his case in the Connecticut Supreme Court, Caldor appealed to the United States Supreme Court, which upheld the store. The sabbath law, said the Court, violated the constitutional principle that government "must take pains not to compel people to act in the name of any religion." The law was struck down by an 8–1 vote, with O'Connor joining the majority.

In 1987, the Court ruled that states may not require public schools to teach "creation science" (a religious theory holding that, less than 10,000 years ago, God created the universe and all its life forms in 6 days). In a 7–2 vote, the Court invalidated a 1981 Louisiana law that required public schools to give creationism as much class time as evolution. The Court's opinion, written by Justice William Brennan, did not claim that creationism had no scientific support. Rather, it said that, by altering school courses to reflect religious views, Louisiana had violated the First Amendment ban against any law "respecting an establishment of religion."

O'Connor concurred in Brennan's ruling, but she also joined a separate opinion, written by Justice Lewis Powell. Powell and O'Connor maintained that school officials should be free to choose courses unless "the purpose of their decisions is clearly religious." Schoolchildren, asserted the two jus-

tices, "can and should properly be informed of all aspects of this nation's religious heritage." Schools, they added, may not use the Bible and other religious documents "to advance a particular religious belief," but they may use such material to demonstrate their roles in history and literature.

Still another school case concerned student privacy. Here, O'Connor took a more conservative stance. In 1985, a New Jersey student sued her high school principal after he searched her pocketbook for evidence of smoking. O'Connor joined the Court majority in a 6–3 ruling against the student. Students may be searched, said the Court, if authorities have "reasonable grounds" for believing that the search will reveal materials in violation of the law or school regulations.

Court watchers have found O'Connor difficult to predict. In 1983, for example, she took a strong stand against a form of censorship. The case began with a newly passed Minnesota "paper and ink" tax, levied primarily on the press. One newspaper, the *Minneapolis Star*, challenged the tax as a violation of the First Amendment's guarantee of freedom of the press. After the Court ruled in favor of the newspaper, O'Connor was assigned to write the majority opinion. Selective taxes of this kind, she concluded, "can operate as effectively as a censor to check critical comment by the press, undercutting the basic assumption of our political system that the press will often serve as an important restraint on government."

In 1984, O'Connor wrote another majority opinion, this one in a labor case, that surprised some observers. The case concerned a group of illegal aliens and their employer. After the workers tried to start a labor union, their boss had retaliated by reporting them to immigration authorities. The move, which put the workers in danger of deportation, raised an interesting question: Should federal labor law protect illegal aliens even as federal immigration law seeks to expel those aliens?

O'Connor said yes. It was not illegal to hire aliens at the time, and she found "no reason to conclude" that the labor policy conflicted with the immigration policy. The employer's action in this case, she wrote, was motivated by "antiunion" sentiments.

Justices are judged not only by the opinions they write but by the opinions they join (or refuse to join). In a number of cases that concern women, for example, O'Connor has joined a Court majority that decided in favor of female plaintiffs. In one, a 1987 case dealing with the promotion of women, she approved a voluntary affirmative action program established by California's Santa Clara County Transportation Agency. At issue was the legality of promoting a female employee to a skilled-craft position over a slightly more qualified male employee.

How did O'Connor, who had criticized sexual discrimination in the Joe Hogan case, explain her vote for the woman's promotion? In the Santa Clara case, O'Connor noted that no woman had ever been employed in any

of the transportation agency's 238 skilled-craft positions. This fact, she said, offered strong evidence of past discrimination and legitimized the agency's modest effort to undo its past wrongdoing.

During her first eight years on the Court, O'Connor wrote opinions on court procedure, copyright, and criminal confessions; on race, employment, and immigration; on oil drilling off the California coast and on land reform in Hawaii; and on the licensing of nuclear power plants. Of all the areas on which she has voted, however, abortion is one of those most closely watched by the public.

The subject arose in her second term on the Court, when O'Connor issued one of her most controversial dissenting opinions. The case involved the city of Akron, Ohio, which had passed a law restricting women's rights to obtain abortions. Recalling its 1973 ruling in *Roe v. Wade*, the landmark case that established the constitutional right to abortion, the Court struck down the Ohio law. O'Connor not only disagreed but launched a heavy attack on the logic of *Roe v. Wade*.

As an Arizona state senator, O'Connor had generally favored liberalized access to abortion. Her dissent in the Ohio case might suggest that she had changed her views, but one must read her opinions in order to understand those views fully. One must also recognize the vast difference between the work of a legislator and that of a judge.

As a lawmaker, O'Connor, quite properly, voted for measures she con-

Opponents on the abortion issue state their case outside the Court in April 1989. The demonstration was one of many sparked by Webster v. Reproductive Health Services.

sidered wise. As a judge, she was called upon to apply the law as written, whether she considered it wise or not. And as a Supreme Court justice, she must decide not whether she approves of a given law or lower-court decision but whether it meets the requirements of the Constitution.

Public interest in O'Connor's stance on abortion intensified in 1989, when the long-running controversy about the subject returned to the boiling point. Two Republican presidents—Ronald Reagan, who appointed O'Connor to the Court, and George Bush, who succeeded Reagan in 1989—had expressed their determination to overturn *Roe v. Wade*. As well as appointing O'Connor, Reagan had filled two Court vacancies with men known to be anti-abortion: Antonin Scalia and Anthony Kennedy. Reagan had also elevated the conservative William H. Rehnquist to the post of chief justice.

Often joining Rehnquist, Scalia, and Kennedy on social issues is a fourth justice, Byron R. White. On the Court's generally more liberal side are Harry A. Blackmun, Thurgood Marshall, William J. Brennan, Jr., and John Paul Stevens III. Between these two groups stands Sandra Day O'Connor, who, observed a *New York Times* reporter in late 1989, "is the only justice not clearly on one side or the other." The justice, noted the *Times*, "holds the key to the constitutional future of abortion. . . . There has been vigorous debate among legal specialists over the direction of her thinking."

Antonin Scalia, nominated to the Court by Ronald Reagan, makes a point during his Senate confirmation hearings in August 1986. Scalia was sworn into office the following month.

Several abortion rights cases came before the Court in 1989. Receiving the most attention was *Webster v. Reproductive Health Services*, which questioned the legality of a Missouri law that placed a number of restrictions on abortion. Conservatives hoped the Court would uphold all sections of the Missouri law, a move that would have eliminated much of the free access to abortion granted by *Roe v. Wade*. Liberals hoped the Court would strike down the whole Missouri law.

Webster was argued in a highly charged atmosphere. All the justices received thousands of letters from both pro-choice and antiabortion activists, but O'Connor, perceived as the swing vote on the issue, got the most. In July, when the Court made its decision on *Webster* public, hundreds of placard-carrying demonstrators assembled outside the Supreme Court building.

A 1989 *New York Times*/CBS poll showed that 41 percent of the population thought abortion should be "generally available," while 42 percent supported stricter controls than currently existed. (Only 15 percent, however, said that abortion should not be permitted at all.) The Court's *Webster* decision showed the justices to be as sharply divided on the abortion issue as the American public itself; in 78 closely printed pages, the Court issued 5 separate opinions.

By a vote of 5–4, the Court upheld much, but not all, of the Missouri abortion law, ruling that the state could prohibit the performing of abortions in public hospitals, forbid the use of state funds for abortion counseling, and require doctors to refuse to perform abortions after the 20th week of a healthy pregnancy.

O'Connor provided the needed fifth vote to uphold the Missouri law, but she angered conservatives by refusing to denounce *Roe v. Wade* in her written opinion. State restrictions on abortion, she said, were permissible as long as they were not "unduly burdensome" to women seeking abortions. She also re-emphasized her belief in the legitimacy of a state's interest in protecting human life. Justice Scalia, who had urged his fellow justices to use *Webster* to overturn *Roe*, showed a rare touch of judicial asperity at O'Connor's moderate tone. In his own written opinion, he called her position "irrational," and said, "[It] cannot be taken seriously."

Abortion, of course, is only one of the nation's enduring and controversial issues. Others—racial justice, freedom of speech and religion, the relations between Congress and the president, the death penalty, the right to impartial jury trials, among many—are also certain to be debated for years at every level of government and, inevitably, in the Supreme Court.

In January 1989, O'Connor issued a highly controversial opinion, this one in a case involving minority-owned construction companies in Richmond, Virginia. At issue was the legality of a Richmond law that called for channeling 30 percent of the city's public works funds into companies owned by

Justices Lewis Powell and Sandra O'Connor prepare to give congressional testimony on Court financial needs. The Court's spending is controlled by the House of Representatives.

black contractors. The Court struck down the law, ruling that it violated the right of white contractors to equal protection. "Racial classifications are suspect," said O'Connor, "and that means that simple legislative assurances of good intention cannot suffice." Fixed, racially linked spending quotas, she concluded, could be justified only if they served a "compelling state interest" by correcting "identified discrimi-

nation" by the government or by private companies. The Richmond law, said O'Connor, failed that test.

Associate Justice Thurgood Marshall, who had spent most of his life battling for racial justice—and who believed the battle far from won—wrote a strong dissent in the Richmond case. Affirmative action programs, he argued, should be judged by a flexible standard, one that takes into account

94

the nation's racial history. "In concluding that remedial classifications warrant no different standard . . . than the most brute forms of state-sponsored racism," he wrote, "a majority of this Court signals that it regards racial discrimination as largely a phenomenon of the past, and that government bodies need no longer preoccupy themselves with rectifying racial injustice."

Thus the Supreme Court's first black associate justice and its first female associate justice found themselves in profound disagreement. But conflicting opinions on the Court have a long and honorable history, and the winner of one battle may well be the loser of the next. O'Connor addressed this subject in a speech to the Women's Club in Chautauqua, New York.

"E. B. White [the American essayist] once said, 'Democracy is based on the recurrent suspicion that more than half the people are right more than half the time,'" O'Connor told her listeners. "In the narrow view, the Supreme Court is based on the suspicion that five justices are similarly correct," she continued. "If you do not agree with all of the Court's holdings, you are certainly not alone. But you may be confident that we never stop trying . . . to contribute appropriately to the fragile balances of our national democracy."

O'Connor receives an honorary law degree—one of many bestowed on her since she joined the high court—from the University of Minnesota Law School in 1987.

EIGHT

"Women Should Involve Themselves"

American women have made significant progress in the past few decades. A living symbol of that success, Sandra Day O'Connor has become one of the nation's most influential public officials. But as she herself has said, women have yet to achieve full equality, in the field of law as elsewhere. In the nation's law firms, for example, about 30 percent of today's young associates are women—but only 5 percent of the firms' partners are women. Fewer than 5 of every 100 members of Congress are women, and women also constitute less than 5 percent of U.S. judges.

According to a 1989 poll, conducted by the *National Law Journal* and the West Publishing Company, America's female lawyers continue to face obstacles specific to their sex. The majority of the women surveyed said they were paid as well as their male counterparts but that their personal life had suffered because of their career; many said they had felt forced to choose between marriage and their job. Almost half the women said they had delayed having children in order to advance in their profession; of those who had taken maternity leave, 43 percent said their career had been hurt by their absence.

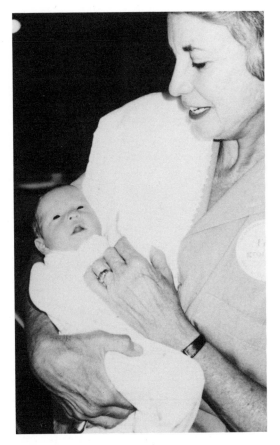

The Court acquires a Courtney: O'Connor cradles her first grandchild, Courtney Day O'Connor. The baby girl was born to Scott O'Connor and his wife in October 1989.

As a young lawyer, O'Connor had faced even more daunting barriers, but she refused to let them stand in her way. Reflecting on her decision to interrupt her legal career for her young children, she once said, "In the long run, nothing was lost. . . . The joy of having our children is one that lasts a lifetime—far beyond one's professional career." Most women, added the Supreme Court justice, "discover that they actually can reenter the profession and they can make up for lost ground."

Today, as she has for years, O'Connor lives three lives: her own, her family's, and the life of the Court. Her husband commutes between a Washington law office and his Phoenix law firm. Often asked if he minds being the less celebrated half of his marriage, John O'Connor explains that he feels great satisfaction in his wife's successes. "After all," he joked to one reporter, "I am president of the most exclusive club in the world—the Men's Auxiliary to the Supreme Court."

In a more serious tone, O'Connor said, "My life has become vastly broadened and vastly enriched as a result of [my wife's] appointment. I am not only happy for Sandra because she is so competent and so deserving, but I am happy for myself and my family because all our lives have become more interesting. Sandra's accomplishments don't make me a lesser man; they make me a fuller man."

The 3 O'Connor sons, now adults, pursue successful careers of their own, and one—32-year-old Scott—presented his mother with her first grandchild, Courtney Day O'Connor, in October 1989. "All have performed very well indeed," O'Connor recently said of her sons. "I see them already taking on jobs as volunteers in some of the things I was interested in long ago. And that's just wonderful to me. I think it's important that young people get involved,

Both Ada Mae and Harry Day, seen here at the Lazy B in 1979, lived to see their daughter become the first woman on the Supreme Court.

B ranch where Day had been a young, uncertain bride 60 years earlier.

Just before the Court's 1988 term began, O'Connor, then 58 years old, learned that she had breast cancer. Two weeks after doctors discovered a malignant tumor, O'Connor entered Georgetown University Hospital for surgery and chemotherapy. Those two weeks, O'Connor later told close friends, were the worst of her life. Characteristically, however, she treated her illness not as a catastrophe but as a challenge. Although some Court observers speculated that she might retire, O'Connor made it clear that she had no intention of quitting.

Before her cancer diagnosis, O'Connor had scheduled a speech at Washington and Lee University in Lexington, Virginia. The date turned out to be one day before she was scheduled for surgery, but O'Connor calmly drove to Lexington and delivered the promised lecture anyway. Immediately after her operation, she released a statement in classic, no-nonsense O'Connor style: "I underwent surgery for breast cancer. It was found to exist in a very early form and stage. The prognosis is for total recovery. I do not anticipate missing any oral arguments." Accurate as ever, she missed no arguments and, in fact, carried a full workload throughout the 1988 term.

O'Connor also kept up with all her usual activities, one of which is checking over the mountain of mail that arrives in her office each day. The letters contain requests for signed photographs, interviews, charity donations,

and I'm extremely proud that our sons are becoming part of community activities."

O'Connor, who had always been as proud of her parents as they were of her, lost them both after she joined the Court. Harry Day, 86, died 3 years after watching his daughter's investiture in 1981. And in April 1989, Sandra O'Connor and her family scattered the ashes of Ada Mae Day at the top of Round Mountain. The site overlooks the Lazy and information about the Court. The justice also receives dozens of invitations to make speeches and to attend social and charitable events, but she can accept only a handful of such offers each year. When the Court is about to hear an especially controversial case, O'Connor receives floods of letters urging her to take one position or another. Like her fellow justices, however, she refuses to allow public pressure to influence her decisions.

Along with her full load at Court, O'Connor often officiates at the swearing in of new federal officials. She administered the oath of office to Elizabeth Dole as secretary of transportation, to Margaret Heckler as secretary of health and human services, and to many other cabinet members, ambassadors, appointees, and judges. "I think," she once joked, "I've heard more oaths than a bartender announcing that it's closing time." In January 1989, she swore in Dan Quayle as vice-president of the United States.

O'Connor herself has been repeatedly mentioned as a possible Republican vice-presidential nominee, a conjecture fueled by her long-standing friendship with President George Bush. The justice, however, has often insisted that she is on the Supreme Court to stay. In October 1991, she will celebrate her 10th anniversary on the bench. During that decade, she has continued to refine both her judicial expertise and her philosophy.

Any good judge decides cases one at a time, applying the law as precisely as possible. To do this, of course, a judge must have a set of philosophical beliefs; Justice O'Connor is surely no exception. As a former state senator, she has a firm faith in the state legislatures and in their responsibility for developing local law. The "dual sovereignty" of America's national and state governments, she has noted, is a novel experiment in the history of nations. Like many other ingenious and complex innovations, the system is fragile and requires tender care. "We must never forget," says O'Connor, "that the answers to many of our deepest national dilemmas may lie not in Washington, D.C., but in the American spirit of ingenuity embodied in lawmaking authority closest to the people themselves: our state and local legislatures."

As a onetime state judge, O'Connor also has deep respect for the state courts. In all cases, particularly criminal cases, she believes that state court proceedings should take priority, and be fully exhausted, before the federal courts intervene in any way. She is convinced that, whenever reasonable, the federal courts should then defer to the earlier decisions of the state courts.

But O'Connor knows the courts cannot answer every problem, and she knows that lawyers, too, are essential in the attainment of justice. In the worst of cases, lawyers can make problems worse instead of better, but, O'Connor believes, good lawyers can contribute much to society. She has urged them to spend more of their time representing the poor. "Too many lawyers are insensitive to their greater ethical and social responsibilities," she

Vice-president Dan Quayle takes the oath of office from O'Connor (back to camera) on January 20, 1989. The justice herself has been suggested as a vice-presidential candidate.

has said, "not because such responsibilities do not exist or haven't been recognized, but because legal education has neglected them." O'Connor is a lawyer herself and for many years included much volunteer work and public service in her practice of law.

O'Connor believes passionately in equal justice for all, black and white, wealthy and poor, women and men. "Society as a whole," she says, "benefits immeasurably from a climate in which all persons, regardless of race or gender, may have the opportunity to

101

O'Connor shakes the hand of her old friend, former Senator Barry Goldwater, at a 1987 Phoenix ceremony marking the 200th anniversary of the U.S. Constitution.

earn respect, responsibility, advancement and remuneration based on ability." Once a victim of gender discrimination herself, O'Connor has learned from that experience, too. "I feel strongly that qualified women should involve themselves more than they do now," she has said. "They should be particularly anxious to seek appointments in government or seek out qualified women for political offices."

Above all, O'Connor believes in the possibility of change for the better. Her first office at the Supreme Court commanded a view of a small brick house, the former headquarters of the National Women's party and home of suffragist Alice Paul. The building, says O'Connor, reminded her daily that barely 70 years earlier, women had yet to win that most basic of civil rights, the right to vote. And, she says, it continues to serve as a reminder "that single-minded determination and effort can bring about fundamental changes in even a well-entrenched system of discrimination."

When she was named to the Court, reporters asked O'Connor to comment on her unique position. "Yes, I will bring the understanding of a woman to the Court, but I doubt that alone will affect my decisions," she replied. "I think the important thing about my appointment is not that I will decide cases as a woman, but that I am a woman who will get to decide cases."

In one poll after another, American women cite O'Connor as a role model; she has, after all, gone where no woman had gone before. Much of her mail is from women who simply want to tell her how much they admire her; in the days following her rise to the bench, she received—and acknowledged— more than 4,000 congratulatory letters. "It's been touching to see how women of all ages have responded to the appointment of a woman to the Court, with an outpouring of appreciation that it happened and a feeling of encouragement that the appointment gave them," O'Connor remarked in a 1985 magazine interview.

The Supreme Court's massive bronze doors, predicts trailblazer Sandra Day O'Connor, will open to other female justices in the near future.

"I had no idea when I was appointed how *much* it would mean to many people around the country," O'Connor told another magazine writer. "It affected them in a very personal way—

Taking a break from the law in 1987, Sandra and John O'Connor explore a section of China's 1,500-mile-long Great Wall, begun in 300 B.C.

people saw the appointment as a signal that there are virtually unlimited opportunities for women. It's important to mothers for their daughters and to daughters for themselves."

Endlessly interviewed about her "secrets for success," O'Connor has given generous credit to the pioneers of the women's movement. "It wasn't until the '60s that women began to bring to the forefront the continuing concerns that they had about equal opportunity," the justice told a reporter in the mid-1980s. "I am sure that but for that effort, I would not be serving in this job."

It is probably safe to predict that there are young women now in high school, college, or law school who will one day take seats on the Supreme Court. A reporter recently asked the first female justice if she believed that women would eventually constitute half the Court. "I surely would think so," replied Sandra Day O'Connor. "In our law schools today at least half the students are women. I fully expect to see the percentages of women in the practice reflected in the roughly similar percentages on the bench and in other activities in which lawyers are generally engaged. So I certainly do think we are going to see that reflected—not only here but in judicial offices across the nation."

Justice O'Connor had arrived on the Court under the full glare of the public spotlight; as she approached the end of her first decade on the Court, she remained the subject of close scrutiny, heated controversy, and what the *New York Times* called "vigorous debate over the direction of her thinking." None of this relentless attention, however, appeared to affect the unflappable rancher's daughter. Serene but deter-

The Seal of the Supreme Court, designed in 1782, shows the American eagle bearing the United States motto E Pluribus Unum, *Latin for "Out of Many, One."*

mined, O'Connor continued to display the crisp independence that had characterized her since childhood. "She held her own," recalled a Lazy B ranch hand who had known her all her life. From all indications, Sandra Day O'Connor would continue to do just that.

FURTHER READING

Bentley, Judith. *Justice Sandra Day O'Connor.* New York: Messner, 1983.

Bodine, Laurence. "Sandra Day O'Connor." *American Bar Association Journal* 69 (October 1983): 1395–98.

Fox, Mary Virginia. *Justice Sandra Day O'Connor.* Hillside, NJ: Enslow, 1983.

Goode, Stephen. *The Controversial Court: Supreme Court Influences on American Life.* New York: Messner, 1982.

Greene, Carol. *Sandra Day O'Connor: First Woman on the Supreme Court.* Chicago: Childrens Press, 1982.

Lawson, Don. *Landmark Supreme Court Cases.* Hillside, NJ: Enslow, 1987.

Rierden, Anne B. *Reshaping the Supreme Court: New Justices, New Directions.* The Impact Series, edited by Margaret Ribaroff. New York: Watts, 1988.

Woods, Harold, and Geraldine Woods. *Equal Justice: A Biography of Sandra Day O'Connor.* Minneapolis: Dillon Press, 1985.

Woodward, Bob, and Scott Armstrong. *The Brethren.* New York: Avon Books, 1981.

CHRONOLOGY

March 26, 1930	Born Sandra Day in El Paso, Texas; spends early years at family's Lazy B ranch on Arizona–New Mexico border
1946	Graduates from high school in El Paso
1950	Graduates magna cum laude from Stanford University
1952	Graduates third in class from Stanford Law School; becomes deputy county attorney in San Mateo, California; marries John Jay O'Connor III
1954	Begins two-year stint as civilian lawyer for U.S. Army in Frankfurt, West Germany
1957	Gives birth to first of three sons; opens law practice in Maryvale, Arizona
1965	Becomes an Arizona assistant attorney general
1969	Appointed to Arizona State Senate
1970	Elected to first of two full terms in State Senate
1973	Becomes Senate majority leader
1974	Elected judge of Arizona Superior Court
1979	Appointed to Arizona Court of Appeals
1981	Nominated by President Ronald Reagan to United States Supreme Court; confirmed by U.S. Senate in September; takes seat as America's first female associate justice

INDEX

Abortion, 16, 41, 55, 56–57, 59, 90, 92–93
Adams, Abigail, 61
American Bar Association, 67
Amicus curiae, 62
Apache Indians, 21–22
Arizona State Bar Association, 51
Arizona State Personnel Commission, 37
Arizona Territory, 21
Austin High School, 27, 28

Babbitt, Bruce, 49
Barr, Burton, 46
Bendheim, Alice, 46
Bentley, Judith, 84
Biden, Joseph, 59
Blackmun, Harry A., 87, 92
Blacks, 79, 94, 95
Bradley, Joseph P., 29, 79
Bradwell, Myra, 29, 79, 83, 84
Brennan, William J., Jr., 87, 89, 92
Briefs, 62
Brown, Marilyn, 28
Brown v. Board of Education of Topeka, 85
Burger, Warren, E., 18, 87
Bush, George, 59, 92, 100

Carswell, G. Harrold, 59
Case conferences, 62
Civil Rights Act of 1964, 38, 82
Committee to Reelect the President, 38

Concurrences, 65, 74
Congress, U.S., 38, 79
Constitution, U.S., 29, 50, 77, 82, 92
  First Amendment, 87, 89
  Fourteenth Amendment, 29, 82
  on nomination of federal judges, 16
  on Supreme Court, 79

Day, Ada Mae (mother), 21, 22, 23, 24, 26, 99
Day, Alan (brother), 25, 26
Day, Alice (grandmother), 21, 22
Day, Ann (sister), 25, 26
Day, Harry (father), 21, 22, 23, 25, 26, 32, 99
Day, Henry Clay (grandfather), 21, 22
DeConcini, Dennis, 13
Denton, Jeremiah, 59
Dissents, 65, 74, 94
Dole, Elizabeth, 100
El Paso, Texas, 21, 22, 23, 24, 25, 26, 27
Engle v. Isaac, 84
Equal Pay Act, 38
Equal Rights Amendment, 41–42, 59

Falwell, Jerry, 16
Federal courts, 49–50, 53, 103
First Amendment, 87, 89
Foreman, John, 46
Fourteenth Amendment, 29, 82

Frankfurt, West Germany, 35
Froeb, Donald, 55

Geronimo, 22
Goldwater, Barry, 37, 49
Governor's Commission on Marriage and the Family, 37
Guitierrez, Alfredo, 40–41

Haynsworth, Clement F., 59
Heckler, Margaret, 100
Hogan, Joe, 82–83, 90

Justice Department, U.S., 13

Kennedy, Anthony, 62, 92, 93
Kennedy, Edward, 16
Koch, Mark, 48

Las Cruces, New Mexico, 23
Lazy B ranch, 21, 22, 23, 24, 25, 26, 32, 33, 56, 99, 105
Life Amendment Political Action Committee, 16
Lordsburg, New Mexico, 25
Lynch v. Donnelly, 87

McAlmon, Hondey Hill, 27–28
MacGregor, Ruth, 77
McGrory, Mary, 59
Manzo, Flournoy Davis, 25
Maricopa Board of Adjustments and Appeals, 37
Maricopa County Republican Committee, 37

Maricopa County Superior
Court, 45
Maricopa County Young Re-
publicans Club, 37
Marshall, Thurgood, 79, 85,
87, 92, 94–95
Mexico, 21
Moral Majority, 16

National Association of
Women Judges, 51
National Organization for
Women, 16
Nixon, Richard, 38, 59

O'Connor, Brian (son), 37
O'Connor, Courtney Day
(granddaughter), 98
O'Connor, Jay (son), 37
O'Connor, John Jay, III (husband), 32, 33, 35, 37, 38,
48, 49, 56, 98
O'Connor, Sandra Day
on abortion, 16, 41, 55, 56–
57, 59, 90, 92–93
admitted to Arizona bar, 35
appointed to U.S. Supreme
Court, 13–19, 53
as Arizona assistant attorney general, 37
on Arizona Court of Ap-
peals, 50, 51
as Arizona state senator,
38, 56
birth, 23
cancer surgery, 99
childhood, 23–27
on Constitution, 77
as Court of Appeals judge,
49–51, 53
education
college, 28–29
elementary, 24, 25, 26, 27
high school, 27–28
law, 28–29, 30, 32–33
on Equal Rights Amend-
ment, 41–42, 59

in Europe, 35
financial assets, 55–56
first job, 33
letters to, 100, 103
as majority leader, 38–43
marriage, 33
opinions
on abortion, 90, 93
on Arizona Court of
Appeals, 50, 51
on censorship, 89
on labor, 90
majority, 74, 84, 90
on prisoners' rights, 84
on racial issues, 93–94
on religion, 87–88, 89
on school matters, 89
on women, 90
opposition to, 15–16
in private practice, 36–37
as Republican, 16, 37, 38,
100
Senate confirmation hear-
ings, 16, 56–57, 59
Senate confirmation vote,
16, 59
on sexual discrimination,
43, 84, 90
sexual discrimination
against, 16, 33
and *Stanford Law Review*,
31–32
as Superior Court judge,
45–49, 53
swearing in, 18–19
typical workday, 69–70,
72–73, 74–75
as volunteer, 37, 51
voting record in Arizona
legislature, 41–43
on women's opportunities,
103, 104–5
on women's rights, 41–43,
103, 104
O'Connor, Scott Hampton
(son), 36, 98
Order of the Coif, 31

Park City, Utah, 35
Pasadena, California, 21, 22
Paul, Alice, 104
Phoenix, Arizona, 13, 35
Phoenix Historical Society,
37, 51
Powell, Lewis, 89
Precedents, 65

Quayle, Dan, 101

Radford School for Girls, 24,
26, 27
Reagan, Ronald, 13, 14, 15,
53, 92
Rehnquist, William H., 33,
73, 92
Republican party, 15, 37, 38,
49, 100
Roe v. Wade, 57, 90, 92, 93
Rose v. Lundy, 84
San Francisco, California, 22
San Mateo, California, 33, 35
Scalia, Antonin, 62, 92
Scott, Dred, 79
Senate Judiciary Committee,
16, 56, 59
Sexual discrimination, 16, 29,
33, 43, 79–84, 90
Smeal, Eleanor, 16
Smith, William French, 13, 33
Socratic method, 29
Stanford Law Review, 31–32
Stanford University, 22, 28,
29, 31, 33, 51
Stevens, John Paul, III, 87, 92
Stewart, Potter, 13
Supreme Court, U.S.
blacks on, 79
on *Bradwell* case, 29
on *Brown v. Board of Edu-
cation of Topeka*, 85
cases chosen by, 61, 62
computerized transmission
of opinions, 67
Constitution on, 79
cross-examination by, 29,

31, 73–74
on *Engle v. Isaac*, 84
on *Lynch v. Donnelly*, 87
opinions of, 65–67. *See also* O'Connor, Sandra Day, opinions
oral arguments before, 31, 72, 73–74
on racial discrimination, 79, 93–95
on religion, 87–89
on *Roe v. Wade*, 57, 90, 92, 93
role, 49–50
on *Rose v. Lundy*, 84
on schools and students, 85, 87, 89
on sexual discrimination, 29, 79–84
on *Thornton v. Caldor*, 88–89
on *U.S. v. Frady*, 84
on *Webster v. Reproductive Health Services*, 93
woman appointed to, 13, 15, 16, 18, 19, 53, 55, 59

Taney, Roger, 79
Thornton v. Caldor, 88–89
Tierney, David, 41
Tobin, Tom, 36, 37

United States Reports, 74
U.S. v. Frady, 84

Vermont, 21

Webster v. Reproductive Health Services, 93
White, Byron R., 92
Wichita, Kansas, 21
Wilkey, Ada Mae. *See* Day, Ada Mae
Wilkey, Mamie Scott (grandmother), 24, 25
Wilkey, Willis (grandfather), 22, 24
Women
discrimination against, 29, 43, 79–84, 90
in law, 33, 36, 97, 106–7
opportunities for, 102, 104–5
rights of, 38, 43, 79–82

PICTURE CREDITS

Peter Huber is a lawyer and writer. After graduating summa cum laude from Harvard Law School, he clerked on the District of Columbia Circuit Court of Appeals for Judge Ruth Bader Ginsburg and then on the U.S. Supreme Court for Justice Sandra Day O'Connor. He is a Senior Fellow of the Manhattan Institute for Policy Research. The author of several books on law, Huber has written articles for scholarly journals (including the *Harvard Law Review* and the *Yale Law Journal*), magazines (*The New Republic, Science, Regulation*), and many newspapers. He has appeared as a legal expert on "Face the Nation," the "MacNeil/Lehrer NewsHour," and numerous other television and radio programs.

❖　❖　❖

Matina S. Horner is president emerita of Radcliffe College and associate professor of psychology and social relations at Harvard University. She is best known for her studies of women's motivation, achievement, and personality development. Dr. Horner serves on several national boards and advisory councils, including those of the National Science Foundation, Time Inc., and the Women's Research and Education Institute. She earned her B.A. from Bryn Mawr College and Ph.D. from the University of Michigan, and holds honorary degrees from many colleges and universities, including Mount Holyoke, Smith, Tufts, and the University of Pennsylvania.